"Great read for any leader want to get outstanding results honoring their personal values an authentic EMPOWERMENT culture.

Carol C.,
Director, Customer Excellence

-

"Usually, organizations promote people into leadership because of their excellent performance as a 'doer'. Then they don't require or offer leadership training. The Ten Tips to Empowerment Leadership is excellent guidance for all those on their journey from 'doer' to 'Empowerment Leader'."

Max E Rumbaugh, Jr
Executive Vice President Emeritus
Society of Automotive Engineers International

-

"Focusing an organization on its 'responsibility to serve' as Ten Tips to Empowerment Leadership demonstrates, as modeled from the CEO, through the teams, and grounded in individual service orientation is surely a contrasting foundation for success in our modern culture. The Gross family shares their personal experiences and their own paths to purposeful personal and professional relationships through this highly meaningful narrative."

Dr. Ginger MacDonald
Founding Director, Educational Leadership
University of Washington Tacoma

"In my 40 years in the transportation industry, I have experienced all manners of the good, the bad, and the ugly in leadership behavior. The Ten Tips to Empowerment Leadership is spot-on in describing the what and the why of poor leadership behaviors. More importantly, "the how" to improve those behaviors to empower your team. As Jeff and his family say, **emPOWER-ON!***"*

Edward J.
Engineering Manager,
North America Region, Automotive Manufacturer

-

"As a campus leader of a school, reading The Ten Tips to Empowerment Leadership just solidifies my own quest for becoming a great leader. Education is on a precipice and the only way we can handle the challenges we face every day is to connect powerful leadership with compassion, heart, vulnerability, patience, and a growth mindset. I can't wait to share this with my district."

Kristin M. Albaugh,
Principal
Midland Independent School District

"The Ten Tips to Empowerment Leadership – information that is essential to being successful as a business professional."

Michael "Sully" Sullivan,
President and CEO
ACEC Georgia

TEN TIPS TO EMPOWERMENT LEADERSHIP

TEN TIPS TO EMPOWERMENT LEADERSHIP

The POWER of PEOPLE FIRST

*By Jeff Gross,
Dr. Maria Gross,
Tabitha (Gross) Claus,
Jacob Gross*

Published - October, 2022

Jeff Gross, Dr. Maria Gross,

Tabitha (Gross) Claus,

Jacob Gross

All rights reserved. Except for brief quotations in critical publications or reviews, no part of this book may be reproduced in any manner without prior written permission from Gro-Nova Inc.

gro-nova.com

PAPERBACK ISBN: 979-8-3573-1696-7
eBOOK ISBN: 979-8-3573-1696-7

Manufactured in the USA

 linkedin.com/in/mbajeffgross

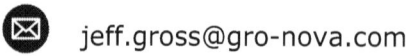 jeff.gross@gro-nova.com

Dedication

We dedicate this book to all the great, and not so great leaders, we had in our lives from whom we learned so much, and now share with you.

Thank you for all that you taught us!

emPOWER-ON!

Contents

	Preface	XI
1	Self-Serving to Other-Serving	1
2	Lorded Over	7
3	The Mother of Empowerment Leadership is Servant Leadership	15
4	Personal Values Matter	20
5	The Why of Empowerment Leadership	38
6	Why Won't You Stay?	47
7	Creating an Empowerment Leadership Culture	55
8	Empowerment Accountability	79
9	REI of Empowerment Leadership	88
10	Listening is Serving	112
11	But Wait There's More!	122
12	What NOT to do as an Empowerment Leader	126
13	Remote Working: The Perks and Pitfalls of Working at Home	136
	The Last Thought	147
	About the Family of Authors	149

Preface

"emPOWER-ON!"

Jeff Gross

emPOWER-ON! My first professional leadership opportunity came within a year of graduating college. I was a Shift Supervisor in a manufacturing plant and the youngest of a 17-person crew. To say I made every mistake imaginable would be a "HUGE" understatement. One of my favorite responsibilities during an annual plant maintenance outage was to lockout the main electrical power supply. There was only one main power source that controlled the power to the entire plant. I remember the "POWER" I felt every time I would switch the main power supply back on.

You would have to push hard on the electrical breaker switch to make it move to the "ON" position. Then it would make a loud click, a thud, and finally the buzzing of electricity. The hairs would stand up on my arms. I can still feel the excitement and empowerment today! I always had a big smile on my face when I announced over the plant two-way radio - "The Power Is ON!"

"You need the team way more than they need you."
Jeff Gross

The only other experience I had during my first leadership role that brought me such energy, excitement, and joy was when I was able to switch on the team's empowerment switch. It took me about a year to gain their respect and figure out that I needed the team way more than they needed me. Once I dropped the "boss act" and stopped being a "know-it-all," the empowerment switch was "ON". I began to respect their input and ask their opinions on everything from operational concerns to crew performance issues. They felt empowered and so did I.

We became an empowered team and our results showed it. We soon became the best performing team in the company. We were having fun, learning from each other, and exceeding our performance numbers. The team empowerment switch was "ON". It was "emPOWER-ON!" from there on for the team.

I learned that surrendering my own selfish needs and putting my "People First" changed everything for the better for both the team and my career. The team's productivity improved - my team and I were both growing professionally - there was a greater team connectedness, autonomy, and trust. I was recognized and promoted for being an outstanding leader by not leading at all, but by serving my team.

"Empowerment Leaders realize that an Empowerment Culture is the engine that drives success."
Jeff Gross

Effective leaders empower their teams to be and do their best. My family and I firmly believe that everyone is a leader in one way or another. Whether professionally or personally, we all have a sphere of influence. Learning to be an authentic, other-serving, empowering leader can and will change lives. The *Ten Tips to Empowerment Leadership* is a work of passion, dedication, and love of leadership. We share what we have learned, studied, and lived, so you can become an Empowerment Leader and change lives also. Maria, Tabitha, Jacob, and I have each held leadership positions from an early age and we believe that you are born to lead, but you just don't know it yet.

It is our hope, desire, and passion that you will learn the power of Empowerment Leadership. Empowerment Leaders realize that an Empowerment Culture is the engine that drives success. That putting your "People First" matters to meeting every imaginable goal you may have as a leader and company steward. Read on and be empowered to empower your team!

emPOWER-ON!

CHAPTER 1

Self-Serving to Other-Serving

"I have been blessed to have been managed by such awful, egotistical, self-destructive, abusive, self-serving leaders that I became one myself."
Jeff Gross

What makes me an expert on Empowerment Leadership? You see, I have been blessed to have been managed by such awful, egotistical, self-destructive, abusive, self-serving leaders that I became one myself. To understand the importance of changing your leadership mindset we need to understand how we can lose our way.

My journey, like many of us, to becoming an Empowerment Leader started as a child. We need to understand that not only do we mimic the behaviors of our leaders today but we mimic the behaviors of our first leaders; our parents. Scary thought, I know. I was raised in a lower middle-class family in Detroit where I learned that money was supposed to buy you love & happiness. I know now that is not true, but that's what I learned growing up. My father had a crummy job, with crummy pay, working crummy hours, for a crummy greedy boss. My two brothers and two sisters along with my mother were also living it. My father would get called into work at all hours of the day, night, weekend, and holidays. Before picking up the phone he would say under his breath "son of a bitch" then put on a smile and say "hello, I'll be right there" and off he went.

My mother wanted us all to be financially successful and blamed her unhappiness on not having enough money. She instilled in us that education plus ambition would lead to money, security, and happiness. My parents managed to scrape up enough money to buy a tiny cottage on a lake in Michigan and I would sit on my mom's lap as we looked at the large beautiful expensive houses across the water. She would say,

"Jeffrey, they put on their pants the same way that you do and if you get an education and work hard you can have that too."

Now don't take me wrong, I would not be here today with the successful career, big house, nice car, and beautiful wife and kids if I hadn't had that vision instilled in my psyche. The issue in my life was I would achieve that success at any cost. I was afraid of failing, being unhappy and poor, and living on the wrong side of the lake. I was living every moment of every day as though I would lose it all. This fear was driving me to be a fearful self-serving jerk. Every decision I made was through the lens of how this will benefit me first, not the company and definitely not my team. I was professionally immature, scared, and lacking a healthy personal value system.

> "Jerks help Jerks be Jerks."
> Jeff Gross

I have learned that I'm not the only one. Our culture praises the strong, ambitious, and cutthroat leaders. People are promoted on results only and not how they achieved them. Power hungry, dominant, dictatorial, hierarchy organizations feed the ego, school the wicked, and drive fear of losing it all. I was professionally immature and I didn't want to lose my so-called success identity. I quickly learned that the traditional power hungry, dominant, dictatorial, hierarchy organizations would reward me for being a power hungry, dominant, dictatorial, self-serving leader. Go figure. Many ask how jerks get promoted while nice people don't? What's wrong with the question is that only nice people ask this question. The jerks know exactly why this is the case. The answer is plain and simple; jerks help jerks be jerks.

In my career, I worked for a couple of large fortune 500 companies. I was ambitious, greedy, egotistical, and self-serving. I didn't have the best interest of the companies, employees, or our customers. I put my self-interests first, second, and third. I saw a clear pathway for advancement - pleasing my boss and hoping he would throw me a promotional bone. I came to work every day with the goal of impressing them. In doing so, I lost my own internal-values compass and took on the poor management characteristics of the bosses that were higher than me in the power-dominant organization.

> "Most hierarchical organizations reward their leaders who kiss the butts of the people above them and kick the butts of the people below."
>
> Jeff Gross

I became so fearful of losing my position that I lost who I was. I was a puppet of the people I worked for and that was just fine with them. They were also fearful of losing their position and were puppets of their bosses. On-and-on the story went - up the corporate "I'm King" hierarchical ladder. Our self-worth was determined by the organization's hierarchy. We were personally defined by our titles, position, and pay. Fear and pride drove every leadership decision consciously or unconsciously. My and others' gut-check was not what was best for the customers, employees, or company but what was best for me, myself, and I. The ladder rewarded and punished based on fear. It was a kiss butts, kick butts mentality. You would kiss the butts of the people above you in the ladder and kick the butts of the people below you. Do this enough times and you move up the ladder. Refuse to do it and you would soon be moved down or out. Simple rules; tough game.

You may think that you have a hierarchical organization that is not based on pride and fear. You feel that your organization is serving your employees and customers to the best of its ability. Well, if that is true, you are one-in-a-million, your turnover rate is below 5%, your employee satisfaction is above 90%, and your customer return rate is through the roof. Oh, almost forgot, your Trust Leadership Indicator is above 90%.

Bravo, you have not fallen trap to the outdated top - down - hierarchy - bureaucracy - me - me - me - first - & - always - you - last - every - time - shut - up - I'm - King Hierarchy leadership model. For the 99.999% of you left, please read on. For the .001%, you need to write a leadership book.

CHAPTER 2

Lorded Over

"I wasted years of my life trying to please the King, only to be lorded over."
Jeff Gross

A 2021 Gro-Nova poll showed 65% of workers feel their company tolerates the bad behaviors of its leaders. There is an inherent flaw to the "I'm-King" Hierarchy model. It is too easy to be king or a lord over all. The energy of the organization is misdirected away from your employees and customers and focused upward toward the nobility. It is human nature to take advantage of the position, power, and prestige of the kingdom. The top-down hierarchy is intoxicating and addictive. I wasted many years of my life trying to please the king only to be lorded over myself.

I'm King Hierarchy Model

I had the position, money, prestige, and pride. According to the world and my mother I should have been happy; instead, I was miserable, empty, and unfulfilled professionally and personally. I hated the people who I was working for and was a total fake. My life and actions revolved around feeding the fear and pride of the top echelon. The ladder demons were ruling my life. I wrote the following poem to give you a small glimpse into the madness.

> Demon of Pride, Demon of Fear
> All the things I hold so dear
> My pride, my addiction, my personal friend
> Deep in my soul, you'll be my end
> *by Jeff Gross*

I needed to change what I was acting like and find who I really was. My poor leadership heart was filled quickly by poor bosses and I needed a heart transplant. I had to break the chains of fear to become a better person and better leader. I needed to fill my new heart with my own beliefs and values and not someone else's.

How I fell so easily into becoming a power hungry, dominant, dictatorial, self-serving leader was a lack of strong personal values. My mother instilled a semi-worthy vision of success, but not the values that dictated how it will be achieved. The values that made up my heart were rotten and needed to be replaced. I valued prestige, arrogance, money, and pride. I wasn't being corrected in the "I'm-King" Hierarchy companies I worked for. On the contrary, I was being rewarded with prestige, arrogance, money, and pride. I was achieving outstanding results, but at what cost. I'll tell you at what cost. Everything!

Personally, I was depressed, exhausted, highly anxious, and paranoid. Professionally, I was a short sighted, hurtful, untrustworthy tyrant, and a total jerk. My bosses loved me, while the people who mattered hated me. Another poem I wrote that touches on the state I was in:

> Know your heart and know yourself
> Who do you think you are
> Empty heart quickly filled
> Quickly falls apart
>
> *by Jeff Gross*

The following is a true story. Because I was lacking a heart with a strong personal value system, I was kindly given a new heart by my manic, depressive, narcissistic boss. Because I wanted success at any cost,

I bought it at top dollar. Above market value and way more than I could emotionally afford. To protect the guilty, I have changed his name. His name was Rob but let's call him Ralf. Ralf wanted what I wanted. He wanted to be professionally rewarded and moved up the ladder. He had something to prove and I was professionally immature enough to do his bidding. My heart was empty and up for grabs. He saw that and quickly filled it with his rotten values.

He valued control, power, and manipulation. He put on a smiling, caring face to the team then made me stab them in the back. I began to realize I was becoming someone I was not. I started to question what I was doing and if the cost was too high. How badly did I really want success and did the results outweigh the means? I was professionally growing up fast and realized this was not what I wanted. I thought to myself, "if this is what it meant to be a leader then I didn't want anything to do with it."

Once, I was working nights and got called by Ralf to shut down a piece of finishing equipment prior to the morning shift for maintenance. I was suspicious that something was up because maintenance never required us to shut down at night. This created a backlog in production that was eventually worked through and counted on the following day's production report. Ralf had fooled the system that allowed him to set a new production record for the following day. We all received a coat and personal letter from the CEO. The Operations Manager knew it was a lie but looked the other way. There were 166 employees that refused to wear the coat because it was based on a lie. I donated my coat to Goodwill.

I asked myself why this man was allowed to stay a leader. There were warning signs everywhere that this tyrant was awful to work for. I threatened to quit four times in two years. One manager quit after two weeks working for him. The executive leadership team brushed it off as he never wanted the job in the first place. I was thinking "RIGHT!". This guy never wanted the job, that's why he moved his family 1000 miles to come work for us and quit after two weeks. The executive leadership team was protecting his poor behavior because of his good results.

Ralf was allowed to get away with murder because his results were good. Matter of fact, his results were great. Best in the company. He led with such a heavy hand that people were in constant fear of reprisal and being publicly chastised. He was too valuable to the company to get rid of. He was never even counseled on his poor behavior, as far as I know. It definitely didn't change if he was.

So, I did what 70% of employees do when working for a tyrant; I quit. I decided to leave once I found out that the company values, even though they stated they valued integrity, empowerment, compassion, and respect, were not being lived.

> "It matters how you get results."
> Jeff Gross

Every company has a Vision, Mission, and Values statement. They wear it like a badge of honor. Only when asked what the company's values are, does leadership spit them out with pride and self-serving authority.

Our Vision
is to be the leader in innovation and services.

Our Mission
is to be a world-class industry provider and to deliver the highest value to our customers.

Our Values

are to be self-serving, feed the fear and pride of our organization structure, and to lie, steal, and cheat our way to the top.

(Well, this is what I saw anyway.)

Most companies are true to their Vision and Mission statements. Not so true when it comes to its stated values. Values reflect the heart. How can a company have a heart? I refer to values as the non-negotiables. It matters how you get results, how you treat people, and how you live. The sad part is there are many leaders who feel that a heavy hand is necessary to achieve results. They believe employees can't be trusted and our customers want to rob us blind.

They couldn't be more wrong but it's understandable because they were raised by the "I'm King Hierarchy Organization." I have found that there is a better way to get outstanding results and save your heart. I remember when I first learned about Servant Leadership; the foundation of Empowerment Leadership. It was one of those ah-ha moments in my life.

CHAPTER 3

The Mother of Empowerment Leadership is Servant Leadership

> "The result of Servant Leadership is an empowered team"
> Jeff Gross

I discovered that Servant Leadership is the opposite of the top - down - hierarchy - bureaucracy - me - me - me - first - and - always - you - last - every - time - shut-up - I'm - King Hierarchy leadership model.

In *The Servant Leader*, Ken Blanchard explains

that Servant Leadership is an organization mindset change that places your clients and employees at the top of your organizational hierarchy. Thus, forcing the organization to serve them first. He goes on to explain that Servant Leadership is a matter of the heart; a transformation from seeing everything through the eyes of self-interests to the eyes of other-interests.

I'm a Servant Hierarchy Model

I see Servant Leadership as a heart transplant to a new healthy heart of high character and strong values. A heart that wants to serve our employees' and customers' needs before our own. A heart that is reflective of who I am personally and one that I wanted professionally. A heart transplant was my opportunity to be an authentic Empowerment Leader.

I saw that I was misguided and misinformed. My rotten values were leading me to poor decisions for short-term gains and literally killing me mentally and physically. I now felt I had a choice to be the type of leader I wanted to be and not what others dictated to me. It felt like I professionally matured overnight and my heart grew two sizes that day. The decision to be other-serving not only saved my professional career, but also resulted in my most rewarding and enjoyable experiences of my professional life.

I found that the result of Servant Leadership is an empowered team. Taking what I learned about Servant Leadership, applying it, building strong relationships, engaging with the team on decision-making, and motivating them to be their best resulted in a self-directed, high-performance, power-house team. Thus, Empowerment Leadership was born.

Learning how to empower the team resulted in not only great results but a team that was motivated, felt respected and listened to, empowered to make decisions, and, for me, I was leading with my authentic self. Win-Win-Win! For the company, team and myself. Now that's Empowerment Leadership.

Our Ten Tips will help you become an Empowerment Leader too, while avoiding being a jerk. Our first tip gets right at the heart by flipping your organization hierarchy upside "UP".

TIP #1

Flip your organization upside UP:
The upside is happier people,
clients and profits

Flipping your organization upside "UP" requires you to stop serving yourself and start serving others. For most, this is easier said than done but once your Empowerment Leadership switch is turned "ON" you'll never turn it off. By focusing on the needs of the people who are actually making things happen, your organization will slowly improve its culture resulting in increased employee engagement, satisfaction, and retention, while ultimately improving client loyalty and experience. Changing the energy and focus of the organization toward your employees and clients will require you flip the direction of organizational power to your People First, not the CEO.

You will need to be well-suited for the resistance to change that you'll be faced with. You will need to know and live out your personal values. Your personal values, or non-negotiables, are necessary and matter in creating an Empowerment Leadership culture.

CHAPTER 4

Personal Values Matter

"Our values should be valued."
Jeff Gross

Why do people do what they do? How can leaders fall so far from grace? Why are some leaders awesome and others awful? Your answers may be different to these questions but the root cause is the same; our personal values affect how we act. Personal values will determine what kind of leader we will be. They matter and having strong personal values is critical to being an Empowerment Leader.

Personal values determine who you are as a person and, when demonstrated, show your character and how you'll connect to and treat other human beings. Values influence what you say and think, and drive your positive and negative actions toward others. Values have a moral and human relationship imperative (Alshammari et al, 2015). People do not know who you truly are until they see your values in action. Your lived-out values define your character and will be remembered when you are long gone. Will that be a good or a bad thing for you? Our values should be valued and determined by us and not someone else. Thus, Tip Number 2.

TIP #2

Know and LIVE-OUT your
Personal Values

It goes without saying that a person's character is influenced by our lived-out personal values. Character is a measure of a person's choices in life that either positively or negatively affects people. Our actions reflect our values, character, and ultimately our heart. Many of us take our values way too lightly. Our values should be known and valued. We need to decide what our values are and how we will act before the world puts our values to the test. And believe me, leadership will put them to the test.

Too often we will act in conflict with our values only to afterwards say we'll never do that again. Then later, we will make the same mistakes again and again and again. Why do we find it so difficult to live our values? I feel there are three reasons we don't live-out our values.

First, we don't know what they are. Have we really hashed out our personal values? Have we put them on paper and placed them on our refrigerator? I find many leaders have not and those who have are not revisiting them nearly enough. I personally never even thought of personal values until I was in my first job after college. During the on-boarding process I learned about company values. I thought to myself they sounded like personal values. The company valued integrity, safety, respect, and pursuit of excellence; all noble pursuits. I learned in my first 30 days that the only person who even knew what they were was the On-Boarding Facilitator. No one else in the company was living them, let alone knowing what they were.

> "I was asking what their personal values were to get to know each team member, but they did not know themselves."
> Dr. Maria Gross

In my (Dr. Maria) first month as Director of Teacher Education, I met individually with each of my team members, asking them to list three personal values and why they were important to them personally and professionally. After the first meeting, where the team member could not verbalize even one, I realized I needed to provide time for them to consider the values that guided their lives. I was asking what their personal values were to get to know each team member, but they did not know themselves. After each was able to articulate their personal values, we began to grow our team and I was able to better support each team member. We built our community of trust; knowing our own and each other's values.

> "Your culture is defined by the worst behaviors of your leaders - not the best."
>
> Jeff Gross

Second, we are not held accountable for poor lived-out values or expected to live-out good values. Many organizations put their culture on the back burner to aggressively get results. Your culture is defined by the worst behavior of your leaders, not the best. Then when the culture deteriorates, they act all surprised. Oh-so-often in our professional lives people and organizations will just look the other way when leaders demonstrate poor behaviors.

A 2021 Gro-Nova poll showed 65% of companies tolerate the bad behavior of their leadership team. Two-thirds of companies will choose to accept the poor actions of their leaders in the name of profits. They'll justify their actions by saying "oh, Jack is just having a bad day and Jill didn't mean it." I have seen this first-hand myself. The results of such egregious tolerance are not only appalling but results in a toxic unhealthy work environment that is costing you millions, if not billions, in disenfranchised employees.

> "As Empowerment Leaders, if we are not creating a culture of treating people well then, we are condoning poor behavior."
> Jeff Gross

Poor lived-out values are so apparent throughout our lives that it becomes the standard operating practices of many organizations today. Outbursts, not listening, over-demanding, inflexibility, and zero engagement are just a few of the bad behaviors that can destroy a company culture. As Empowerment Leaders, if we are not creating a culture of treating people well then, we are condoning poor behavior. We become complacent and numb on how we treat others and believe if we live by a higher standard, and buck the system, not only will we not succeed but we won't survive.

> "In this dog-eat-dog world we will act like dogs."
> Jeff Gross

Lastly, we don't decide or train ourselves on how we will act ahead of time in tough situations. Life comes at us fast and under pressure we will act like the way we think others think we should. In this dog-eat-dog world we will act like dogs. A thousand times, I have experienced leadership meetings where one bad apple will spoil all the rest by blurting out "I feel we should fire them!" No one dares to challenge that person in fear of losing their job in their stead. We need to know our values and how we will act ahead of time when these situations come up.

Like a trained professional, we need to train off the field so we know what to do on the field. If we are going to be people of character, we need to decide what our personal values and character are before we get on the field.

I used to lead a production team. Once, there was a severe accident where a team member was stuck in a piece of equipment. His arm was badly injured and I remember how I panicked. The blood rushed to my head, my heart jumped out of my chest, my legs became weak, and I froze up for what seemed like an eternity. Luckily, another operator flew into action and I finally calmed down enough to act.

I made it through it and so did he. Later I

analyzed my reaction to determine what I would do better next time. I needed to plan ahead of the event so I could properly act. Like any well-trained athlete, firefighter, soldier, or leader we need to know how we will act before we need to.

Unfortunately, a year later I was tested again with another injury on my crew. I quickly and effectively moved into action. I have lived this moment before and knew exactly what I needed to do because I already decided how I would act. I was pleased that I had taken the time to determine how I would act before I had to. I also learned that safety, like culture, needs to be emphasized daily.

For me, determining what your non-negotiable personal values are and how you will act ahead of time is the same thing. When you're put in sticky situations you already know what you will and will not do. You need to roleplay and plan what you will say and do if:

- You are asked by management to go against your values.

- You see others do something against your values.

- Your organization does not value what you value.

"Educate first"

Dr. Maria Gross

I (Dr. Maria) faced a sticky situation and was grateful I had recently reviewed my non-negotiable value that a situation should be viewed as a learning opportunity, not a means to condemn. A team member was repeatedly being challenged by a student who asked questions with answers available in an orientation. The team member was becoming short in her email responses to the student. I was asked by my supervisor to "sunset" her (i.e., fire her politely) when complaints went to upper management. But we needed the team member's expertise so I relied upon my value "to educate first" and asked the supervisor to let me work with her and give her another chance.

The supervisor begrudgingly concurred. I knew the supervisor would come back to me if the situation was not resolved quickly. I asked deeper questions about the situation, the student, and each one's reactions. The team member and I began a critical incident reflection to determine if there were hidden biases and how the situation could better be addressed (BranchED, 2021; Howard, 2003).

After critical reflection, we determined the changes needed: the student was to view the orientation again, I was to add additional clarifications to the orientation, and the team member was to pause after writing and delay sending email responses when upset. In addition, training was completed for all team members where others shared similar situations. We all grew together because we took the time to learn from the situation and not negatively react. I stood firm to my personal values, in spite of a supervisor's strong request that I fire the team member.

"All the good or bad in the world can be traced back to someone's lived-out values."
Jeff Gross

Through all the schooling and leadership training I've (Jeff) had, none of them has addressed what I believe in personally and how my leadership style and decisions are affected. In my MBA ethics classes, we learned what we shouldn't do, but not why would we even think of doing them in the first place.

I have done things in my life professionally and personally that I am not proud of. It's only been through maturity and self-reflection that I have come to realize how much personal values matter in every aspect of my life. All the good or bad in the world can be traced back to someone's lived-out values. There is an old saying that if you don't stand for something you'll fall for anything. If you don't determine what your values are, someone else will. Most often that will not be a good thing.

> "I feel the truth of the matter is personal values trump company values – good or bad."
> Jeff Gross

As I progressed up the corporate ladder, I became more aware of the importance of personal values in company decisions. My ambition, greed, and immaturity were warping my values to serve what was best for me. I didn't make decisions under the so-called company values matrix but my personal values matrix. I may have pledged allegiance to the company, but I was serving myself. I believe this is true for many leaders whether they admit it or not. I feel the truth of the matter is personal values trump company values; good or bad. If we don't decide to value our values, then our lived-out values will be thrown to the corporate wind of poor leadership decisions. We need to value our values. We need to own them and make them our non-negotiables.

"Most company values are a list of beautiful words and ideas that are a measuring stick of organizational dysfunction."
Jeff Gross

We don't show up to work in the morning and hang up our personal values to put on company values; even if we remembered what the company values are. I worked for a company that under every light switch was a list of company values. My office mates and I would come in after meetings and cross out the company values that weren't being lived-out. It didn't take us long to blacken out the whole list.

I find that many companies' upper management create their company values in a vacuum. They are ceremonially walked to the Board where they are reviewed and destroyed further. Then, lastly, edited again by marketing to serve potential customers and investors. Most company values are a list of beautiful words and ideas that are a measuring stick of organizational dysfunction. The cultural battle between the dream and reality of lived-out values not only leads to increased disengagement but the eventual demise of the company.

"Companies don't have values, people do."
Jeff Gross

All of our leadership actions add up to decide the company's culture; not what is in the company's beautiful brochure. You can think of a company's culture as the addition of:

Company Vision + Company Mission + Company Values = Company Culture

Similarly, you can think of a person's character as the addition of:

Personal Vision + Personal Mission + Personal Values = Personal Character

I don't see the deterioration of either personal character or company culture from their vision or mission but from their innate value system. Specifically, the good or bad personal values lived-out in the company or personal life. Companies don't have values, people do. Therefore, in my mind the company culture is the addition of:

Company Vision + Company Mission + "PERSONAL" Values = Company Culture

"Your culture is determined by the poorest personal values of the leadership team."

Jeff Gross

Personal values matter more to our company culture than company values. Without values our

Leader-"Ship" is rudderless. Without strong personal values, we will be acceptable to the over-dominating poor leader's values in the organization. Additionally, the culture is determined by the poorest personal values of the leadership team. One bad apple does spoil the lot. Ralf was allowed to get away with his poor personal values lived-out in the company by others on the leadership team. Therefore, the whole company was judged by his actions.

I was easily manipulated as a leader because I felt the company encouraged and rewarded management not on their stated company values but their demonstrated values. I finally determined that I had enough of being someone else's puppet and needed to live-out my "OWN" personal values.

I decided to determine what my personal "non-negotiable" values were going to be. I asked myself, "what kind of leader did I want to be? Better yet, what kind of person did I want to be?" As I reflected on the poor decisions I made and how easily I was manipulated as a leader, it hit me that I cared too much what others thought of me. I was so focused on what people thought that I was ruled by fear and was a self-serving, dysfunctional leader. I was excessively inwardly focused and self-serving.

All of my decisions were through the lens of me, myself, and I. If "I" was going to become an Empowerment Leader "I" wanted to be, then "I" needed to stop thinking about "I" first and start thinking about YOU FIRST. I needed to build my personal values around putting *PEOPLE FIRST*.

I remember a cartoon I saw years ago that went something like this:

IIIIIIIIII - do you want to talk about - me me me me me me me me me

What an Idiot

That is who I was - the guy on the left. Mr. I Me.

I decided that for me I needed a Leadership Vision, Mission, and Values reset. I needed a heart transplant. I based my personal values on some that I had and some I inspired for. I reflected on lived-out values of friends, family, and peers, both good and bad, and determined that:

My Vision
is to serve others over myself to bring them joy.

My Mission
is to share what I have learned so far and
to continue to learn.

My Values
are Honesty, Respect, Kindness,
Trust, and Teamwork

If I had my personal values established prior to working with Ralf, I believe I would have had the courage to stand up for my beliefs. Maybe I would have never taken the job in the first place; I was warned about Ralf during my job interview. During the facility tour, a soon-to-be coworker told me not to take the job because Ralf had serious issues. I wanted so badly to move up the ladder that I convinced myself it wasn't as bad as I was told and that I could handle it. I was right, it wasn't as bad, it was worse, and I was wrong, I couldn't handle it.

"When your team doesn't know your values, they will assume you don't have any."
Jeff Gross

I feel we overlook and don't value our values. We need to ask ourselves what kind of leader do I want to be? Better yet, **WHAT KIND OF PERSON DO I WANT TO BE?** Knowing what our non-negotiables are before we enter the business war establishes our rules of engagement. We hold ourselves personally responsible and know our walking-away-point.

Our hearts are filled with the values we value and not what others value. When we determine what kind of leader and person we want to be, we are truer to ourselves and our Empowerment Leadership heart. When your team doesn't know your values, they will assume you don't have any. Many leaders will say they value this or that but if you are not communicating and demonstrating your values then your team will wonder what your values truly are.

CHAPTER 5

The Why of Empowerment Leadership

> "The utopia of leadership is an Empowered Team."
> Jeff Gross

The Why. Why does Empowerment Leadership matter? Why should we change how we treat each other and the people we lead? Why should we take a hard look at ourselves and change our mindset toward putting our People First?

Not only is empowering the team the right thing

to do as a human being, but, lucky for you, by treating your people right you'll be rewarded in more ways than you'll ever know. Higher engagement, lower employee turnover, a culture of trust, company growth, greater sense of community and improved employee self-esteem and well-being, increased motivation and competence are just a few of the many benefits of an Empowerment Leadership mindset.

I don't have to show you the multitude of studies that have shown how workplace stress, depression, and chronic disease is on the rise. I don't have to show you because I, and many I know, lived it firsthand. A leader who leads in fear will raise the fear of the organization. Fear begets stress, stress begets mistrust, mistrust begets misery, misery begets fear… and on and on the broken management cycles goes.

Empowerment Leadership matters today more than any other time in my over 20-year leadership career. The company-first pendulum has swung too far toward the company, thus leaving employees disheartened, mentally drained, disengaged, untrusting, and scared of what the future will bring.

A 2021 Gro-Nova LinkedIn Poll showed that 53% of employees don't trust their boss. We have seen for almost 30 years a constant year-over-year deterioration of company and leadership values. Leadership fraud, greed, discrimination, devaluing people, benefit and compensation reductions, reduced retirement 401K matching, pension elimination, pay stagnation, and the constant threat of employee cutbacks have led to increased leadership mistrust and organizational fear. The lack of employee sense of control and the feeling of being undervalued have led to greater mental health and performance issues.

Gallup and Harris employee polls have stated that nearly:

70 Percent
of employees are not engaged.

70 Percent
of managers don't engage.

70 Percent
leave because of their boss.
(Percentages are close approximations to actuals of 72%, 69% and 75% respectively)

Year-over-year the polls tell us the same thing. I've found that most leaders feel the polls are incorrect, not reflective of their organization, and/or don't know what to do about it. I call this phenomenon the 70:70:70 Conundrum. As Empowerment Leaders, we need to listen to what our people are telling us or just live with the 70:70:70 Conundrum at our own peril.

TIP #3

Know your NUMBERS

Annual Retention Rate
(100%-Turnover Rate)

Annual Trust Index
(Percent of Employees who "TRUST" their -
Executive Leadership, Direct Manager,
and Peers)

Empowerment Leaders know their Annual Retention Rate and Trust Index. I feel these two measures alone are key indicators of your culture and leadership opportunities. Many companies will rely on employee surveys, but I find most are confusing and don't really tell you what you need to know as an

Empowerment Leader.

I worked for an organization where each year we would debate how the poor results from our yearly employee surveys were from the way the survey was conducted, and not how we conducted ourselves. We debated not what we could do better, but the validity of the poor results of the survey. Literally, we spent hours discussing that the way the questions were asked must have resulted in the poor results. There is no way we could be as bad as people say we are. Well, they were right. We were not as bad as they said, we were worse. After two years, we fired the company that was doing the employee surveys and just put up with good people leaving every year.

"Soliciting team voice throughout the year engages the team and permits leaders to improve and better serve their team and organization based upon immediate needs - not waiting until the end of the year, when it is too late."
Dr. Maria Gross

My (Dr. Maria) institution also uses annual

surveys. When I read the results, I am not surprised. Instead of annual surveys, I focus on feedback surveys after every meeting, project, and significant milestone. A quick four-question, anonymous survey provides immediate input on areas of improvement to make corrective actions or give accolades.

I ask my team the same questions: how well did we meet our goals, what went well, and what opportunities do we have to do better. Appropriate changes are made with the team, who see their input is making our culture and community better.

Soliciting team voice throughout the year engages the team and permits leaders to improve and better serve their team and organization based upon immediate needs; not waiting until the end of the year, when it is possibly too late.

> "Retention starts right from the very first second a new employee is onboarded."
> Jeff Gross

I (Jeff) feel employee retention should be expressed not with the percent of people leaving over a year, but the percentage of people staying. I'm often surprised by how many leaders do not know their retention rate. Retention Rate is a clear indication of your culture and leadership effectiveness. We can debate what your retention rate should be and there are definitely industries with inherently lower retention rates.

A Gro-Nova 2021 poll showed 51% feel a 90% retention rate is an indicator of a poor culture. For most companies, a 90% retention rate is a warning sign. 95% and above you are doing well; below 90% you have an opportunity to create a culture that not only meets the needs of your people, but your clients as well.

Retention starts right from the very first second a new employee is onboarded. When I worked for that tyrant boss, during my first day on the job, I called my wife and told her to stop unpacking. I'm quitting. Yes, he was that bad.

He was a self-serving narcissist with a mean streak and a foul mouth. I stayed there for two years before I finally had enough. I went to the CEO several times, complaining of his unprofessionalism and the way he was demeaning the team. The CEO did absolutely nothing. He just looked the other way because his "perceived" results were good. Yeah, he made his numbers, but at what cost? Our employee retention rate was only 80%, morale was at an all-time low, trust was zero, and employee well-being was null.

Leigh Branham, author of *The 7 Hidden Reasons Employees Leave,* revealed that 89% of bosses believe employees quit because they want more money. In reality, only 12% do. When are we going to realize the cost of poor leadership? I have personally seen executives justify people leaving by putting the cause on the employee. Who else could be to blame! They'll say "it was just not a good fit," "they really didn't have their heart in it," and "they never wanted the job in the first place."

Additionally, the Annual Trust Index also gives excellent insight into a company's culture and leadership effectiveness. The index is the measurement the percentage of your employees who trust:

- The Executive Leadership Team

- Their Direct Manager

- Their Peers

The simple calculation of the number of "yeses"

over the number of people who responded to the poll will quickly indicate if there is a trust problem. I find most organizations have a hard time getting above 60%. Don't be surprised if it's 40%. Of course, the Trust Index needs to be done anonymously to get honest results.

Trust and retention go hand-and-hand and are the culmination of all the good and bad that you do as a leader. Empowerment Leaders have the opportunity to positively influence both these culture indicators.

CHAPTER 6

Why Won't You Stay?

"Understanding why people stay is more important than understanding why they leave."
Jeff Gross

I once left a job and the CEO came to me and stated that if he knew I was unhappy he would have found other opportunities for me within the company. He shared how disappointed he was that I was leaving and felt personally responsible. The company was a $2 billion Fortune 500 company with over 2000 employees. There was another job there for me if I had only shared how unhappy I was in my current role. This really hit me and I swore I would never leave a job again without telling them ahead of time. I also swore that I would ask the people who worked for me that they would do the same. Tip #4 is a proactive approach to people leaving without you knowing why.

TIP #4

Know why people STAY - not LEAVE

Empowerment Leaders perform at least once a year Stay Interviews in addition to Exit Interviews and Individual Development Plans. I recommend and do them twice a year and more often if a team member is at risk of leaving. I feel understanding why people stay is more important than understanding why they leave. Just like the name refers, a Stay Interview is done while a team member is still a team member and is an opportunity to have a good old fashioned, and always rare, heart-to-heart on why people stay.

Finding out in an Exit Interview why someone is unhappy is too late to convince a good employee to stay. Additionally, reactively seeking an employee's feedback when they are leaving could lead to misleading information. Why would I want to kick the beehive on the way out when anything I say will be used against me?

On the contrary, Stay Interviews not only give insight on what improvements need to be made to your culture and work practices, but allow your team members the opportunity to make a positive contribution to that change. Especially if you listen to what they are telling you. And listen you should.

The following are a few best practices recommended by Indeed to keep in mind when conducting Stay Interviews:

Best Practices for Stay Interviews

- Don't combine Stay Interviews with performance reviews to ensure that the focus is solely on the employee's work experience and needs.

- Ask questions that address both the positives and negatives of an employee's position as well as questions about working for the company as a whole.

- When changes are made, let the employees who

contributed to the changes know and show appreciation for their input.

- Do not dismiss or trivialize an employee's answers or opinions even if you do not agree with them.

Ilan Mochari from Inc. magazine also recommends that the Stay Interview be done informally between just the direct manager and the team member with the goal of understanding why people want to work for you and what would make them want to leave.

There are many questions you can ask but Dr. John Sullivan suggest from his *"Stay Interviews: 20 Possible Questions You Should Consider Asking"* and I recommend that you consider asking at least these 10 questions during your Stay Interview:

1. Tell me specifically, what factors cause you to enjoy your current job?

2. If you were asked why, you stay working here what would you say?

3. Do you feel that you are currently doing "the best work of your life?"

4. What factors could contribute to you "doing the best for your life?"

5. Do you feel that your work makes a difference in the company? Our clients? In the community?

6. Do you feel "fully utilized" in your current role?

7. If you were given the opportunity to redesign your current role, what key factors would you include in your "dream job?"

8. What are the most challenging but exciting aspects of your current job?

9. Highlight any recent recognition and acknowledgment that you have received.

10. If you were to ever consider leaving, please help me understand what factors might cause you to leave?

I always add an additional request, not a question. I ask, "if you are planning on leaving, please let me know before you do. I would like to have the opportunity to find you a position here that would make you happy." That request alone could make someone want to stay. It would have for me.

At the end of the interview, you are accountable for the information you've learned and the corrective actions. Thank them for their honesty and time. Summarize what you've learned. Brainstorm potential corrective actions with them. Include them in solving the problem they have brought up. Use the information gathered to make positive changes toward creating an Empowerment Leadership culture.

> "Stay Interviews should not wait until after the first year. They should be a regular part of the feedback cycle from Day 1."
>
> Dr. Maria Gross

I (Dr. Maria) wish my supervisor had met with me to discuss these questions when I had first started a new position with a new organization. I accepted a job without a job description, a big warning sign, but was honored that they "created" the position because of my skill set. Upon arriving, I learned that the title I accepted, "Director", was now "Coordinator." I had left an Associate Dean position and moved over 1000 miles for this position because of the organization's strong reputation and an opportunity to enact positive change in the teacher education field. I was downtrodden.

I was not even scratching the surface of my skills. So, I tried to talk with my immediate supervisor explaining what I had planned to accomplish based upon discussions during the hiring process. I was told to "wait for a few years - we don't work that fast here". After repeatedly asking for the job description and opportunity to begin projects, I gave up.

I worked my easy job and looked for a challenging new one. I was ready to leave when I found a mentor and shared my frustration. He encouraged me to move past my immediate supervisor and share ideas directly with the leadership team. I found some hope and encouragement. An Exit Interview was diverted. An unofficial leader helped me overcome most of the negative factors that caused me to consider leaving.

A new supervisor, after my previous one left, listens and hears my hopes and plans to support new programs. I am finally doing "the best work of my life." I encourage all to find a mentor if your supervisor is unwilling to complete Stay Interviews.

CHAPTER 7

Creating an Empowerment Leadership Culture

"Values without actions are just
unrealized moral ideas."
Jeff Gross

I feel we are at the pinnacle of a worldwide Character Crisis in our personal and professional lives. Over the years there has been a slow drip of deteriorating values. Through the 80s, 90s, and today achieving results at all costs was and is still very costly indeed. It costs us relationships, our character, and the negative impact on our team's well-being.

A University of Massachusetts report estimates $300 billion dollars per year is lost due to workplace stress in US companies: health care, productivity, and absenteeism just to name a few. In addition, according to the study:

- 40% of job turnover is due to stress.

- Healthcare expenditures are nearly 50% greater for workers who report high levels of stress.

- Job stress is the source of more health complaints than financial or family problems.

- Replacing an average employee costs 120-200% of the salary of the position affected.

- The average cost of absenteeism in a large company is more than $3.6 million/year.

- Depression is the largest single predictor of absenteeism and work-related performance.

- Depressive illness, a common side effect of job stress, in employees is associated with nearly 10 annual sick days.

- For every 47 cents spent on treating depression, another 53 cents are indirectly spent on absenteeism, presenteeism, and disability.

- Insurance data indicates insurance claims for stress related industrial accidents cost nearly twice as much as non-stress related industrial accidents.

The brutal fact is most stress is caused by poor leadership and culture we tolerate (Offerman & Hellmann, 1996). Our hyper-competitive nature drives us to do things we never thought we would. Lying, stealing, and coverups have eroded trust between each other and the companies we work for. This has resulted in employee disengagement, high turnover, and a me-generation of leaders; and for what?

An unfulfilled career of getting richer from the blood, sweat, and tears of the people we lead. It's critical as an Empowerment Leader that we know and live-out our personal values. To create a culture of empowerment we need to communicate and live-out our personal beliefs. Values without actions are just unrealized moral ideas.

> "Your culture is determined by the worst behaviors of your leaders and not the best."
> Jeff Gross

One of the largest challenges you will face when creating a culture of empowerment is others in your organization whose lived-out values are in conflict with your own and the Empowerment Culture you are creating. Your culture is determined by the worst behaviors of your leaders and not the best. I have experienced thousands of times the unchecked bad behaviors of leaders, which are sadly even encouraged. Outbursts, not listening, over demanding, inflexibility, and lack of engagement are just a few of the bad leadership behaviors that undo any good you may be trying to do in creating a culture of empowerment.

> "Empowering your team takes courage."
> Jeff Gross

Creating a positive company culture takes company values created by real people, vision from the top, commitment to do what's right, putting people over profits, calling out bad behaviors, and constant communication with the people who wake up early every day to make things happen. Additionally, and most importantly, empowering your team takes courage. Courage to stand up for what's right, courage to challenge your peers and leadership team to do things differently, and courage to treat people with enough respect to empower them to make mistakes, learn, and grow. Trust me, you will be going against the crowd when you say you want to empower your team. Find your leadership courage and you'll find your Empowerment Leadership.

> "An Empowerment Leader blames themselves first before casting blame on a team member."
> Jeff Gross

Oh, how I would love to go back with the courage and knowledge I have now. To not only take back my bad behaviors and decisions, but to challenge other leaders to do and be better. Before I learned the power of empowerment, in my professional immaturity, I would not stick up for my team when there were mistakes and performance issues. Matter of fact, the leadership team did not expect me to.

It would not take much but a quick comment from a leader during one of our meetings to say "throw the book at them" without blinking an eye. Everyone would shake their heads in agreement, even if they didn't. Then the king would give a thumb down and off rolls their head. Then on to the next topic without any remorse. An Empowerment Leader blames themselves first before casting blame on a team member.

> "In the absence of compassion, ruthlessness will prosper."
> Jeff Gross

In my professional life, my character was under constant attack. In toxic work environments, I felt the pressure to do as I was told or they would find someone else to be the jerk. I was wrongly over-critical, a perfectionist, and adding pressure to get results at all costs. I felt I couldn't do what was right for fear of losing my job, loss of promotion, being judged, not being liked by the leadership team, failing, lost income, and the fear of fear. The fear of the consequences was greater than the fear of doing what was right. I was in a Character Crisis.

> "Leaders should not throw their people under the bus when they are the ones driving it."
> Jeff Gross

Empowerment Leaders accept the responsibility for their team's performance as a reflection of their own performance. Time and time again I've seen leaders quickly throw their people under the bus when they are the ones driving it. Poor leaders would rather protect their poor performance by placing blame on others. They do this for fear of being let go themselves so it's an easy choice for them to place blame rather than accept responsibility. Some of this fear is warranted if the company culture is one of intimidation and firing for mistakes. Some of it is because their arrogance and egos get in the way of them doing the right thing.

Your culture is defined by the behavior of your worst leader; not the best. Their lived-out poor character defines your company's culture regardless of the pretty words printed on the company's walls. The first step in creating an Empowering Culture is to realize there is a company culture problem. The second step is to do something about it. Once the culture is corrected most of your daily woes will be solved.

One of my proudest Empowerment Leadership experiences was where I had the courage to stand up for a team member and show that the issue was not his fault but ours. I was part of a COVID biopharmaceutical production expansion where we tripled our production by adding 30 new people. We trained them, but as you can imagine we had many costly learning mistakes. In one week, we had over a million dollars of lost product due to formulations mistakes.

There was one employee who was continually struggling and was making many formulation mistakes. His heart was in the right place but he was rushing and making simple costly errors. His immediate supervisor wanted to throw the book at him and let him go. He was adamant that he didn't have what it takes to make it. I immediately agreed that we needed to throw the book but not at him but at us. You should have seen the jaws drop in the room.

I went on to explain that his performance issue is our performance issue. It's too easy to let someone go but we have a responsibility to help every team member be successful. I went on and challenged the team to brainstorm what "WE" can do to help him be successful.

I kid you not, it took us all of just 15 minutes to come up with a simple solution to add a quality control check during the midpoint of production instead at the end. Not only did this prevent his mistakes from happening, but others as well. Our Non-Compliance Reports (NCR) dropped overnight by doing this one simple act. The beautiful outcome was the employee in question was never even reprimanded. Once we realized his problem was actually our problem, a "real" solution appeared.

In an Empowerment Leadership culture, the leaders embrace a **People First** mentality. Whenever there's an issue, they look not to place blame, but to place solutions. They ask: What could "I" have done differently to allow my team members to not make mistakes? Is there a system or engineering change that will improve our overall performance and not just the performance of one? The mind-set change from self-serving to other-serving kicks in and an empowerment cultural change occurs. An empowerment People First Culture will take time but won't happen unless we are other-serving and personally accept the responsibility of our team's performance.

> "As Empowerment Leaders, we need to learn to dethrone ourselves and give our power away."
> Jeff Gross

To create a culture of empowerment, we need to first realize we need to transfer our power as leaders to the team. As leaders, we are not only people of influence but power. We have the power to affect people's livelihood, happiness, and well-being. Consciously or unconsciously our team will fear us because of the power we have over their lives. Very few others in their lives can have a greater impact on their happiness, or sorrow.

As Empowerment Leaders, we need to

understand that even if we don't outright see the fear in their eyes, it does exist. This fear will be factored in every decision they make. As Empowerment Leaders, we need to learn to dethrone ourselves and give our power away. We need to put the team at ease that we are not out to get them and that by serving them shows their importance to the success of the organization and ours.

To some leaders, giving away their power is a scary thought because their identity is wrapped up into their title and they love the false feeling of being in control and self-important. Their ego simply won't let them. Anyone who has been in leadership can spot these people from a mile away and knows their management trajectory is pointed straight into the side of a mountain. They may feel they have the whole world but they will learn soon enough, they don't have anything that the team has not graciously given them.

> "Thousands of years of evolution have evolved us into fearful and competitive barbarians."
> Jeff Gross

To be an effective Empowerment Leader, we

need to get our ego in check. Our egos drive our competitiveness, need for control, and our me-first behaviors. Evolution has ingrained our fight-and-flight tendencies that result in us becoming defensive and protective of our powerful leadership positions. To be an effective leader, we need to challenge and defeat our dino-brains. Thousands of years of evolution have evolved us into fearful and competitive barbarians. We would as soon as crush your head with a rock before giving away our power. This may have kept the species alive before Costco but it is way overkill in today's diverse work culture.

> "Your ego blinds you to the truth
> that surrounds you."
> Jeff Gross

As Empowerment Leaders, we need to get our head and heart right and aligned with who we want to be as a leader. Some leaders may wonder why they need to change their hearts if the results are good. Truthfully, I was in the same spot in my career. Lots of money, lots of responsibility, but also lots of employees not engaged, lots of people leaving, lots of sleepless nights, and lots of years shaved off my life. There is a better way to lead through Empowerment Leadership. It's more aligned with our authentic selves versus our barbarian selves.

> "You're no leader if you don't include your team in the decisions that affect them."
> Jeff Gross

One of the first steps to start giving power away is to understand the power of inclusion. Just like you want to feel in control of your life and be involved in decisions, so does your team. This was difficult for me in my adolescent leadership years. I wanted to impress my boss, my peers, and, yes, even my team. Not only did I want to impress everyone but I wanted to be a Superhero Leader. I wanted to fly in and save the day. I thought to myself "now that is what real leadership is about!" Right? Nope, wrong, very wrong! Including your team in as many decisions as you can is a sign of Empowerment Leadership maturity.

Once, I had a team member come to me and

asked why the leadership team made a decision that affects them without including them. I tried to spin it, then realized they were totally right and we were totally wrong in doing so. Of course, there are some decisions where you won't be able to include the team, but the majority you will be able to and should. From that day forward, I solicited opinions and ideas on critical issues from the team before making any decisions. For me, that was an Empowerment Leadership ah-ha moment.

As Empowerment Leaders, we need to put our team's needs before our own. We need to let go of control and power and dethrone ourselves. There are some leaders who feel that empowering or serving the team is a sign of weakness; if they put their people first, they will be taken advantage of and it will be all R&R (i.e., Rest and Relaxation). Empowering your team is not a sign of weakness, but a sign of strength. You will truly see that empowering and serving your team does result in R&R. Not what you think of, Rest and Relaxation, but true R&R of Respect and Results.

Respect: Empowering your team shows that you respect and trust them which will build their confidence, engagement, and dedication.

Results: Team empowerment is all about results. You want an empowered team to strive to be their best, which in turn will result in higher quality products, better customer service, collaboration, innovation, fun, and "financial" results.

I've heard all the reasons why including the team in decision-making won't work before and even thought it myself. This negative leadership mindset is our dino-brains telling us that if we empower the team the company won't need us; we'll become extinct. The truth is you'll be seen in your organization as a fixer of dysfunctional teams, promoted for your team's accomplishments, and marveled at for being a Super Empowerment Leader. Now that is what real leadership is about!

Once I saw first-hand the power of inclusion, I now insist on it in every leadership position I hold and with every team and executive I coach. Every time I throw it out there is always someone on the leadership team that will resist the notion. I'm here to tell you that... you're no leader if you don't include your team in the decisions that affect them.

It's a huge missed opportunity and the root to many of your cultural and performance issues. By including the team in decision-making, you'll gain the trust, respect, and engagement of the team. Inclusion is the cornerstone of Empowerment. Without it, empowerment will only be a dream. With it, you'll shed your barbarian ways and realize the Power of Empowerment Leadership. That leads to our next empowerment tip:

TIP #5

Be purposeful in building
a CULTURE of Empowerment

"The goal of empowerment is to have happy, engaged, and valued employees that
want to be and do their best."
Jeff Gross

A great culture does not happen by itself. As Empowerment Leaders, we need to be purposeful in creating a culture of empowerment. Creating an Empowerment Culture helps the team to find value in what they do, keeps them engaged, and creates a collaborative creative environment built on respect and trust. The goal of empowerment is to have happy, engaged, and valued employees who want to be and do their best. You can definitely create an Empowerment Culture for just your team but the organizations that embrace empowerment will have a greater competitive advantage and make your empowerment journey easier.

The first step in creating an Empowerment Culture is to realize that you need to change your culture. Many will tolerate a poor culture or think it's too big of a task to change. I remember when I mentioned to my manager that I wanted to create a culture of empowerment and he said "who is stopping you." So, who is stopping you? Even the worst leaders will support the idea of a positive cultural change because they know it will help their bonuses; until they realize they are the ones that will need to change. So, if your company is not ready for a cultural change, as the Empowerment Leader of your team, you can create an Empowerment Culture.

"People won't tear down what they help build."
Jeff Gross

With your team, brainstorm what an Empowerment Culture looks like. It's important that you include your team in the visioning of empowerment. Too many organizations will communicate the vision of its culture from on top of the mountain and the people below are wondering what planet you came from. Many will feel they do solicit the team's ideas but I find it is usually a select few and very infrequently. Remember, people won't tear down what they help build.

Ask your team, "what do you think empowerment looks like?" Give a couple minutes to allow them to collect and write down their thoughts and then go around the room to solicit ideas from every team member. Record your results on a white or easel board sticky paper. This will allow everyone to see the results. Continue around the room until all ideas are captured. Then, have the team force rank them. Force ranking will help with the priorities for the action items that will follow.

A good way to rank ideas is 10-4 ranking. Give each team member 10 small sticky pad sheets and ask them to place their sheets next to the ideas they feel are most important. They can vote up to 4 times for a single item and need to use all of the 10 sticky pad sheets. Then, tally the results. This is now the priority for your Empowerment Culture action items.

To me an Empowerment Culture is when:

- Leaders serve the team.

- People are included in everyday decision-making.

- Bad behavior is never tolerated.

- Leaders make time to coach and mentor their team.

- Respect is respected.

- Families are also a company priority.

- Truth and transparency are core values.

- Having fun is non-negotiable.

In an Empowerment Culture, leaders lead with authenticity and serve the team first. The team then responds with improved employee job satisfaction, organizational commitment, and well-being.

Writing down and visualizing what an Empowerment Culture looks like sets the destination. Then the road map to empowerment can be plotted out. Including the team in creating the vision and action items of empowerment is critical, because they won't tear down what they helped to build. Continue to brainstorm action items for each empowerment priority.

"During the hiring process and onboarding it's important that you clearly explain your culture and what behaviors that will 'NOT' be tolerated."

Jeff Gross

There are two other processes that need attention to maintain an Empowerment Culture: 1) hiring, and 2) onboarding. I worked with a large manufacturer with an awesome culture that was degraded over five years because of the new people who came in and not only didn't understand their Empowerment Culture, but were in conflict with it.

People cannot read your mind at any time, but

especially during the hiring process. You also cannot necessarily tell if a candidate would be a good fit into your culture. But they can tell if they are a good fit or not when you explain to them what your culture is like. During the hiring process and onboarding it's important that you clearly explain your culture and what behaviors that will "NOT" be tolerated. When you put the Empowerment Leadership brand on your culture you now have a clear explanation of the attributes of your leadership you expect.

For example, during the hiring process I would say, our culture is built on empowerment where our leaders serve the team and not that the team serves them. Your team members will be involved in all decision-making and you'll be expected as their leader to build relationships, and engage with them daily. Do you feel you could adapt to our Empowerment Leadership culture?"

During the onboarding process, you'll need to train your leaders what empowerment means and the leadership expectations to maintain the culture. Glassdoor reports that employees feel 18 times more committed and 33% more engaged with highly effective onboarding. Don't miss this opportunity to get alignment with your culture from Day One. Even if a leader has had poor behavior issues in the past, setting clear expectations will keep those behaviors at bay.

Your cultural onboarding training should include teaching new hires:

- Your company's non-negotiable values with real-life examples.

- The attitudes and behaviors that are expected.

- Your cultural commitment by a live testimony from one of your executives.

I also recommend that you follow-up with your new hires 30, 60, and 90 days after the training and ask if they are seeing your Empowerment Culture in action. As we mentioned, an Empowerment Culture does not just happen. Empowerment requires vision, training, daily feeding, and nurturing. Creating and sustaining an Empowerment Culture takes time, commitment, accountability, and constant care.

> "If you don't drive your culture, your culture will drive you."
> Jeff Gross

After creating the vision of empowerment and action items, I highly recommend creating an Empowerment Leadership Cultural Advisory Board. This advisory board not only drives change but holds the team accountable for the actions to create a sustainable Empowerment Culture.

A Fun Committee is not an Empowerment Leadership Cultural Advisory Board, nor is the Executive Leadership team. Creating an Empowerment Leadership Cultural Advisory Board not only shows your commitment to a collaborative and open culture, but gives a voice to all levels of the organization in real time. Waiting for another poor employee survey result is too late to make a positive change to your culture. The board not only lives out the values of empowerment but calls out the company's actions and practices that are in conflict with it. If you don't drive your culture, your culture will drive you.

The purpose of the Empowerment Leadership Cultural Advisory Board is to gain a diverse perspective to give guidance and direction to all leaders in order to sustain the culture. The purpose should include tracking cultural action items, communicating frequently on cultural highlights and new efforts, focusing on employee well-being and morale, and calling out the bad behaviors of the leadership team.

The Empowerment Leadership Cultural Advisory Board should be made up of 6 to 10 people from all levels of the organization. The bylaws need to include that all board members have an equal voice and the purpose is to maintain, communicate, and educate the company's Empowerment Culture. Meet once a month and review the action items from your Empowerment Culture action items. You'll eventually get to a point where there won't be much to do. Avoid the trap of stopping to meet. Your presence and commitment are a deterrent to any present and future bad behaviors.

CHAPTER 8

Empowerment Accountability

"Empowerment Leaders call out the bad behaviors of the whole team including the leaders."
Jeff Gross

The acceptance of poor behavior has grounded our personal values down to a nub. Now more than ever we can't just say we are against poor behavior. We need to act to prevent it. Beliefs without actions are just unrealized moral ideas. You don't own your character until you live it. We need to learn to challenge the bad behaviors that are counter to our Empowerment Culture.

TIP #6

Call out the BAD BEHAVIORS
of your leaders

A 2021 Gro-Nova Poll showed that 65% of companies tolerate the bad behavior of their leadership team. Everything from playing favorites, screaming, exclusion, and all forms of harassment. To create a culture of empowerment, your leadership must be held accountable where Empowerment Leaders call out the bad behaviors of the whole team including the leaders. You will not create an Empowerment Leadership culture without setting the expectation that bad behavior will "NOT" be tolerated and following through with calling out the bad behaviors of your leaders and team.

You can see in the "I'm-King" Hierarchy that challenging the bad behaviors of the team can be virtually impossible. The fear of losing your place on the ladder is too great. But once you have established the Empowerment Leadership Hierarchy where your employees and clients come first, it is virtually impossible not to challenge the bad behaviors of the team.

To challenge the bad behaviors of the organization as an Empowerment Leader you'll need to first set the expectation that bad behaviors will no longer be tolerated. You will not need to create a long laundry list of offenses that some will demand. Just tell them that you'll let them know when they have behaved badly. Trust me, they know the difference.

Then, when challenging the bad behaviors of any team member, including leaders, never do it alone. Always bring someone else. During the feedback I like to use what I call the "Smell the Roses Feedback". Let's say you have a smelly issue you are dealing with. I recommend that for every bad "smelly" behavior you need five good "roses" behaviors to cover up the smell while leaving the person feeling respected, encouraged, appreciated, and challenged.

For example, let's say you have a leader or team member who sometimes comes across demeaning when communicating with others. They are knowledgeable and experienced, but this trait is not becoming of an Empowerment Leader. Leaving this behavior unchecked will undermine empowerment. When determining the five good roses you'll be using during your meeting make sure that you have seen them yourself, then be specific, don't inflate them, and practice ahead of time before meeting with this person with your accountability partner.

Smell the Roses Feedback Example

Smelly Behavior: Pat coming across as being demeaning when communicating with others.

Rose 1: Pat's technical knowledge on the Baker project has resulted in increased value to the client.

Rose 2: Pat has always made herself available to support other projects such as the Calpine Integration. Even working overtime.

Rose 3: Pat has worked well on teams and has demonstrated leadership like she did on Baker and Calpine projects.

Rose 4: Pat has been working for the company for over five years and is always passionate about what she does on every project she has worked on.

Rose 5: Pat has expressed that she wants increased responsibilities and over the last year she has taken on increased responsibilities for planning, budgeting, and forecasting for her team.

Before you get started, here are a few suggestions. When setting up the meeting, mention that your accountability partner and you want to meet to share some feedback with them. Don't try to disguise what the meeting is about. If they ask for specifics before the meeting, just reply with "we'll discuss everything with you in the meeting." Don't make the meeting too far out. Try to meet 1 to 2 days out from the invitation. You don't want to create anxiety about the meeting.

The key to the Smell the Roses Feedback is avoiding the word "but" at all costs. Everything before the word "but" will be forgotten. Shoot for five roses. Two or three roses just won't cover up the smell and might even make it worse. You may mention a couple roses in the same sentence to have the feedback flow more naturally.

Lastly a must do, roleplay the feedback with your accountability partner who will be attending the meeting with you. You want to be fully prepared and ready for any pushbacks you might receive. As the accountability partner, make sure to challenge the feedback as you feel the recipient may do. Together you can be better prepared for giving effective and well received feedback. Before we get to the five roses, let me show you why one or two roses won't work.

Just Rose 1 Won't Do:

"Pat, thank you for meeting with us. As part of our Empowerment Leadership culture change, we all agreed that we would share any stinky situations that we see in each other. I definitely would want you to share with me. First, I want to tell you that your technical knowledge was highly valued by the Baker client. They expressed that your automation experience really showed our expertise.

"There is one thing that I and others have noticed that you may want to be aware of. Sometimes you come across a little harsh. I'm sure you don't mean to, but we have seen it ourselves and others are concerned with how this might negatively affect our Empowerment Culture we are creating here. Do you see how you might be perceived this way?"

Ask yourself without looking, what was Rose 1?

Do you see if you were Pat that this meeting is a hard pill to swallow. How do you think we left Pat feeling with just 1 rose?

Now Rose 1 and 2 Won't Cover the Poo:

"Pat, thank you for meeting with us. As part of our Empowerment Leadership culture change, we all agreed that we would share any stinky situations that we see in each other. First, I want to tell you that your technical knowledge was highly valued by the Baker client. They expressed that your automation experience really showed our expertise. Additionally, the team appreciated your support and extra time you did on the Calpine project.

"There is one thing that I and others have noticed that you may want to be aware of. Sometimes you come across a little harsh. I'm sure you don't mean to, but we have seen it ourselves and others are concerned with how this might negatively affect our Empowerment Culture we are creating here. Do you see how you might be perceived this way?"

If you were Pat, what would you be thinking? I would be thinking "BUT" even though it was never mentioned.

Now, Rose 1 Through 5 is No Jive:

"Pat, thank you for meeting with us. As part of our Empowerment Leadership culture change, we all agreed that we would share any stinky situations that we see in each other. First, I want to tell you that your technical knowledge (1) was highly valued by the Baker client. They expressed that your automation experience really showed our expertise. Additionally, the team appreciated your support and extra time (2) as well as your leadership you did on the Calpine project and Baker project (3). Pat, you have always been passionate (4) about working here, and have done the extra work needed to grow professionally such as planning, budgeting, and forecasting for your team (5) over the five years you have been here. We feel you have what it takes to help us achieve our Empowerment Culture we are all wanting.

"There is one thing that I and others have noticed that you may want to be aware of. Sometimes you come across a little harsh. I'm sure you don't mean to, but we have seen it ourselves and others are concerned with how this might negatively affect our Empowerment Culture we are creating here. Do you see how you might be perceived this way?"

This is just an example of how it would go and you'll want to use your own words. By reinforcing the many good behaviors, you have seen, addressing the poor behavior is done professionally, respectfully, and positively. You are leaving the leader feeling good and understanding that change is expected. Additionally, they also see how they are valued and appreciated.

Challenging the bad behavior of your leaders is critical in changing your culture. If you don't, your organization will remain stale and it will be just another company slowly spiraling downward. It takes courage to create an Empowerment Culture. It also takes Relationships, Engagement, and Inclusion or what we call the REI of Empowerment.

CHAPTER 9

REI of Empowerment Leadership

"The Pillars of Empowerment are Relationships, Engagement, and Inclusion"
Jeff Gross

Foundationally, an Empowerment Leadership culture is built on three key elements: 1) building relationships with your team, 2) engaging daily, and 3) including the team in the decisions that affect them. These three pillars of empowerment are what we call the REI of Empowerment Leadership. They are Relationships, Engagement, and Inclusion - the foundations that an Empowerment Culture is built upon.

Being a leader and engineer, I am always looking for practical approaches to solving organizational problems of low engagement, high turnover, and improving poor cultures. All of the tips up to this point, and the following one, can fall in one of these three buckets; having close working relationships with the team, engaging with them daily, and including them in decision-making. These will all build an Empowerment Culture built on trust, collaboration, and inclusion.

As leaders, we can get caught up in the mundane minutiae of running a company that we forget to keep company with the people who make things happen. We just assume that beneath the team's smiling faces they are smiling, but in actuality they are disengaged, distrusting of leadership, and most likely looking for a new opportunity. I know these things because I have been on both sides of the equation; as a leader and being led. To be an effective Empowerment Leader, we need the REI of Empowerment Leadership.

TIP #7

Build RELATIONSHIPS with
your team

Having relationships with your team members is critical to successfully create an Empowerment Culture that improves employee retention, morale, and engagement. We recognize that friendships with your team at work can be tricky if not done correctly. A 2021 Gro-Nova poll showed 83% of respondents believed you can be friends with your team. From the over 1000 respondents from our Friendship vs Relationship Poll, and nearly 100 comments, the main takeaways were:

1. There needs to be clear boundaries between leadership and friendships. As a leader, you can no longer have deep friendships with a team member. It will create jealousy and lines could be blurred.

2. The relationship needs to be with the whole team. Favoritism hurts people's commitment and engagement which breaks the morale of the team. Empowerment Leaders keep the relationship professional and fair, and are respectful to not leave some people out or uncomfortable.

3. If you become too close and lose your objectivity,

all the leadership dynamics will change. You will consciously or unconsciously treat your friend differently than the other team members.

Although a majority of you feel it is possible to be friends with team members, you'll need to understand the pitfalls and draw the line between close friendships and relationships. There is a difference between having personal friendships with people on your team versus having close working relationships. Relationships are built on a better understanding of who the team member is. It's more than just knowing their family status but what they enjoy doing outside of work and their likes, dislikes, and interests. Friendships are much deeper where you share your life on a personal and private level and spend time together doing activities out of work.

I have seen the pitfalls of becoming too close myself. Once, there was a president of a company where I was working who had a very close friendship with a team member. Their families knew each other well and did things together almost every weekend. Then, the team member failed a random drug test and the president had to fire him. We felt he just screwed his best friend and how can we trust him. The sad thing was that the positive drug test result turned out to be caused by a poppy seed muffin he ate.

Another time, a president with close friendships had to lay off several of his friends. Not only was he heartbroken to have to do it but those relationships were never the same again. Some of you may be thinking then why bother having close working relationships with the team if there may be pitfalls at any level of relationships.

As Empowerment Leaders, we want and need to build relationships with our team. These bonds are important to build trust, collaboration, morale, and reduce turnover. You can have great benefits, interesting work, and an awesome job but if you don't take the time to build relationships with your team, you'll never have a fully empowered and engaged team. People don't work for companies; they work for their leader. The difference is we need to build work relationships that work and not personal friendships. This is an important and sometimes sad reality of being a leader.

Statistic after statistic has shown that people leave because of their boss. In my career, I know that was the case. I've found that when relationships are not present it's like a recipe that is missing the main special ingredient. A good leader can do a lot of things right, but will never achieve greatness without the ability to build work relationships with their team.

> "Be purposeful in creating close working relationships."
> Dr. Maria Gross

I (Dr. Maria) have found I need to be purposeful in creating close working relationships with my teams. I am one to go to work, expect others to do their jobs, and go home at the end of the day; keeping work and home very separate. My first job out of college, I was part of a group of newly hired engineers. The company expected us to become friends and even inter-marry, if possible. The company was in a small remote town. Leadership had found that if a new engineer married, they stayed in town. If not... well, the hiring/matchmaking process began all over again. It worked for some, but not for me. Yes, I met Jeff in this small remote town, but I did not stay. It was too hard to keep the work and home lives separate in this friendship model.

Fast-forward thirty years, I was leading a team who acted like family with brothers and sisters who squabbled. I felt like I was a mom, trying to keep them from hurting each other and our organization. I needed to change the team culture. I wanted to have meaningful and productive work relationships between team members and create an Empowerment Culture that improved employee retention, morale, and engagement. So, I purposely began creating opportunities for the team to socialize and for me to individually build relationships. Quarterly meetings included social time over lunch in which we shared key events in our lives. Individual time was purposeful and based upon the team member's interest: a baseball game with Sam's family, pastries and coffee with Bob, or popcorn and a drink with Linda.

We took turns scheduling these regular team and individual social events. We started to look forward to spending scheduled, respectful, and professional time together. To keep it professional, it was scheduled; not spontaneous.

Personally, I needed it on the calendar and planned in advance. If it was not on my calendar, I would not have taken the time needed to grow the team and reduce sibling friction. We learned to discuss our differences and support each other. We were not best friends, but we developed strong positive working relationships. When one team member was promoted, we cheered and were sad to see her go; even though she and her "work brother" had previously squabbled. We created a work family that respected our differences and opinions. Our organization benefitted as did each of us individually. Now back to Jeff and some activities to build stronger work relationships.

Thanks, Maria, I remember those days well. When I took Maria away from the small town, the company refused to throw her a going-away party. Boy, were they mad at Maria and me. Well, I digress.

There are two work relationship building activities that have been very successful for me: Highlight and Circle of Appreciation. They not only build relationships between the team and me, but more importantly, among the team members. They increase both engagement and build relationships.

Highlight

Highlight came out of an activity we did around the dinner table to get the kids to talk to us. They had to give one Highlight and it never could be a lowlight.

Not only did this set a positive attitude, even on tough days, but we were learning about each other and what we liked.

I took the same idea to work with me when I realized I knew nothing about my team. So, either in the first team meeting of the week or individually, I would ask "what was your Highlight over the weekend?" Asking the typical "how was your weekend?" is a closed-ended question and will get you a simple, often shallow, "it was good, how about yours?" response. Resulting in a "they really don't care" feeling. There is nothing learned or shared. Asking "what was your highlight" opens up a discussion that allows you to learn more about what the team member does with their free time and creates deeper relationships.

During one of my workshops when we did the Highlight exercise, one woman mentioned she went wakeboarding. Not only were there some surprised looks, but there were also some "wow! If she can do it, so can I." During the break I loved seeing people immediately going to her to ask her more about it. There were other co-workers in the workshop that mentioned that they had worked with her for five years and never knew she loved wakeboarding.

Another favorite memory was from a team

member who didn't have any highlights from the first three weekends after starting Highlight and he would just say he "liked taking a nap or watching TV." In the fourth week, he said how he and his wife went to dinner and took a long walk in the park so he had a highlight to share. He chuckled and said his wife likes that we are doing Highlight.

When doing Highlight during a meeting, I recommend going around the room and having everyone give a highlight. They need to keep it short after all it is Highlight, singular, and not Highlights plural. I also recommend doing it every week. Highlight is a fun, simple, and effective way to build relationships.

The Circle of Appreciation

The Circle of Appreciation came out of The Circle of Love that I also would do with our kids. The kids were fighting and our son said he didn't love his sister. I replied, "don't say that and yes, you do." He of course responded "no, I don't." So, I said "OK, everyone get in a circle and we are going to do a Circle of Love." They looked at me like I was from outer space. We went one direction telling the person to the right that we loved them, then the other direction, then crisscrossed matching our daughter and son. First, it was time for our daughter to tell her brother that she loved him, which she did, his defenses dropped, and he returned with "I love you too," a hug, and tears started to flow with all of us. There is power in hearing the words "I love you." Within your family, it can never be said enough. Within your team, it is also the case.

Of course, we didn't go around and say "I love you" to each other, which by the way I do, but we would go around, and say what we appreciated about each other. I started doing The Circle of Appreciation for the same reason I did the Circle of Love with my family.

I had team members who said that they hated each other. Not to each other's faces, but to me and other team members. When they were in the room, you could feel the tension and our performance suffered because of it.

I still remember the first time we did the Circle of Appreciation, how we joked that we would need to get back later to the other on what they appreciated. You felt the love when people shared how they sincerely appreciated the other. When it came to the two who were in conflict, to be honest I was worried about what they would say to each other, but they each had something sincere to say about the other. It took time for their relationship to fully improve, but this was the beginning point.

There are of course other team relationship building activities that you can do and could even come up with your own. The key to me is that it should be weekly. To have a monthly or larger spaced activity does not lead to as strong of working relationships like it does when done weekly.

Do you see the difference between personal friendships and work relationships? Being friendly builds close working relationships while being friends can build divisions and jealousy within the team. Doing both relationship building activities also helps you accomplish the next tip, which is the E in REI; to Engage with your team.

TIP #8

Engage with your team DAILY

"To get engagement, you have to give engagement."
Jeff Gross

Gallup's year-over-year engagement poll reports

that nearly 20% of employees are not fully engaged with 70% being only partially engaged. Additionally, Harris reports that 70% of managers are uncomfortable engaging with their teams. These are two statistics that are not only alarming but ultimately need to be hit straight on.

This is our responsibility as an Empowerment Leader. Increasing manager engagement and employee engagement provide huge opportunities to improve productivity and your competitive advantage. Whether you define engagement as the strength of mental and emotional connectedness; being involved in, enthusiastic about, and committed to what one does; or the level of an employee's psychological investment in their organization, one thing I know for sure is that to get engagement you have to give engagement.

SHRM (Society for Human Resource Management) has reported that higher levels of engagement promote retention, foster customer loyalty, and improve company performance. They go on to say that employees want to feel valued and respected, know that their work is meaningful, and their ideas are heard.

As mentioned, Harris has reported that 70% of leaders are uncomfortable engaging with their team. As an immature leader, I also struggled with engaging with my team. As many of you leaders have experienced yourself, leadership can be a scary endeavor. I remember the anxiety and self-doubt I had before leading a team meeting or a one-on-one session.

According to Healthline, as high as 82% of leaders have feelings of being an imposter. Imposter Syndrome is alive and well in today's leadership. Healthline states Imposter Syndrome involves feelings of self-doubt and personal incompetence that persist despite education, experience, and accomplishments and, I'll add, gender and race. Imposter Syndrome affects many leaders and is a hindrance to engaging with your team. These pressures take a toll on your emotional well-being, as well as your team's, and need to be eliminated.

Highline recommends that you should:

- Avoid giving in to the urge to do everything yourself - Involve the team.

- Challenge your doubts by asking yourself whether any actual facts support these beliefs.

- Avoid comparing yourself to others.

I've suffered, and sometimes still do, to Imposter Syndrome that I realize I must control. My Imposter Syndrome came from an early age when I felt I was not as smart as my siblings and was harshly criticized for mistakes. My journey to becoming an Empowerment Leader is also one of overcoming my self-doubt. I had to stop caring and fearing the opinions of others and needed to dethrone my parents. Don't take me wrong, I love my parents, but I needed to realize, like myself, they are people with imperfections and misdirections.

Once I started to become more of an Empowerment Leader, my engagement level increased and leading became easier. When I let down the boss act and started to lead with authenticity, honesty, and transparency and transferred my power to my team; leading became more engaging, with better results, and more fun. Win-Win-Win! Quantum Workplace has identified six drivers of employee engagement that have the greatest impact:

1. Leaders committed to making it a great place to work.

2. Trust in the leaders of the organization to set the right course.

3. Belief that the organization will be successful in the future.

4. Understanding of how individuals fit into the organization's future plans.

5. Leaders value people as their most important resource.

6. The organization makes investments to make employees more successful.

These drivers are common sense, but when you are caught in your uncommon sense of self-doubt in a common poor organization's culture, poor engagement, well-being, and results will prevail.

Healthline's first recommendation to overcome Imposter Syndrome states you should avoid giving in to the urge to do everything yourself. One of my biggest hurdles and breakthroughs to becoming an Empowerment Leader builds upon this recommendation, which is our next tip; including the team in decisions that affect them. We'll discuss that more shortly, but first let's discuss how to engage.

Start Your Day Slow

To engage with our teams daily, I've learned that you need to start your day slowly and engage before you become disengaged. With me, the day used to start at 4 AM with me lying in bed checking my emails. My mind was already churning on what the day was going to look like and I was already setting my daily priorities. None of which was engaging with the team. I was absorbed by the time-sucking, mostly non-critical, email trap. I still remember a time years ago, OK decades ago, when I would get a work email and people didn't expect a response until the next day or later. Now it's expected we respond to emails almost instantaneously. As Empowerment Leaders, we need to break this habit and make a new one by starting slow.

Start the day slow by not getting to work, or even while lying in bed, and jumping immediately into answering emails. Emails not only pull you away from important work, but pull you away from engaging with your team. When you show up to work, don't dock your laptop right away, but put it down and go make a round and say "good morning" to each team member and ask them "what do you need from me today?".

I once coached an executive of a manufacturing

facility and he said one of his greatest breakthroughs in building an Empowerment Culture was when I recommended, he take a morning round every day on the shop floor. He was hesitant at first when I wanted him to start slow. He even started too fast instead of starting slow. He said at first, he would rush through his morning walkthrough and, at best, take 15 minutes. He shared that he was concerned about the emails that were waiting for his response and he was too busy to start slow. But "slowly" people would approach him more and more when they saw him coming every day and asking "what do you need from me today?" Suggestions for improvement came flowing in.

He was gaining the respect from his employees who hardly saw him before and he was empowering the team by listening and implementing their ideas. Win-Win. His quick 15-minute walkthroughs grew to a slow hour each day which he said he wouldn't give up for the world. Engaging with the team and our next tip of including the team in decision-making go hand-in-hand.

TIP #9

INCLUDE the team in decisions
that affect them

Once after an executive leaders meeting, a decision was made that affected my team. I was in my first director role and my first executive leadership meeting. I went to tell the sales team and our best sales person, Kim, who later I grew to appreciate her intelligence and bluntness. Kim, lol, blasted me with both barrels at close range. She said, "why would you make a decision that affected us without first including us?" I, of course, did what any poor leader would do and I spun it. She wasn't buying any of it and I finally realized she was 100% right and I had no excuses. I apologized and told her I would never do it again. She didn't buy that either and I had to earn her and the team's trust.

It turned out that when I later tried to include the team in decision-making, I was discouraged from doing so from the CEO, who specifically told me not to. I was shocked by this huge "red flag" which I soon learned was a cultural problem that almost put us out of business. Many leaders are fearful of including the team in decision-making because they will lose power and control. They feel that they will be giving away the keys to the inmates and it will be all R&R (Rest and Relaxation).

As discussed, empowering your team by including them in decision-making will be R&R but not the Rest and Relaxation you might be thinking of. But the R&R&R of Respect, Relationships, and Results. When we include the team, we are showing them that we **R**espect their contributions which builds close working **R**elationships and ultimately leads to better **R**esults. R^3 is Empowerment in action.

As a leader, our Ego, fear of losing our job, respect, and control all come into play when we choose not to include the team in decision-making. We need to face down our demons and understand that everything we fear will come to fruition when we don't include the team. As leaders, we need to reflect on why we feel this way.

As an immature leader, I too would not include the team in decision-making and looked for opportunities to solve the problem myself and be the Superhero. Because of my insecurities of being judged for not knowing, of losing my job, or being seen as an imposter, I tried and wanted to do it all myself.

Even now when I share my story, I'm embarrassed that I felt that way, which is one of the reasons I'm an Empowerment Leader consultant today; to save other leaders from being an ineffective false leader and to save their team from having to work for them. Empowering your team matters more today then ever. Together we can emPOWER-ON!

> "If you as a leader are uncomfortable with including the team in decision-making, you need to come to terms that it's not their inability to handle it, but yours."
> Jeff Gross

Learning to trust the team to be involved in decision-making alone was my greatest Empowerment Leadership breakthrough that broke everything wide open for me as a leader. This not only changed who I was as a leader, but also as a person. I started to enjoy leading, or should I say following, or should I say SERVING, the team more. I also felt a huge sense of relief that I didn't have to go around and be a know-it-all hard ass; being a know-it-nothing was a whole lot easier. If you as a leader are uncomfortable with including the team in decision-making, you need to come to terms that it's not their inability to handle it, but yours.

> "Stop being a Superhero and start being a Superleader."
> Jeff Gross

As leaders, we often feel we are paid the big bucks with the big titles and therefore need to be a know-it-all. We'll storm into the boardrooms and slam on the table and shout "I know what we need to do." Yikes! You wish! We need to stop being a Superhero and start being a Superleader. Empowerment Leaders are other-serving; not self-serving. We put our people's needs before our own and ideas before our own by including the team in decision-making. We buck the Conventional approach for the Decision-Maker approach. Skip Prichard contrasts the two approaches below.

Conventional Approach:

- More than 95% of important decisions are made by official leaders.
- Decisions are made or "approved" by leaders at the highest practicable organizational level.

- Bosses ask subordinates for advice, but make final decisions themselves.

- Managers see their role as managing people and resources.

- Bosses see themselves as initiators, creators of vision, developers of action plans, accountability officers, and those who have an ability "to get things done." What I call the Superhero Leadership Syndrome.

The Decision-Maker Approach:

- Some 99% of all important decisions are made by non-leaders.

- Decisions are made by non-leaders at the lowest practicable organizational level.

- Allow team members to manage resources and make decisions.

- Leaders see their role as serving other employees.

- Leaders are mentors, coaches, teachers, helpers, and cheerleaders.

Shifting from the Conventional to the Decision-Maker approach is the right way to do business. By including the team, you are not only creating an Empowerment Culture, but you are getting diverse perspectives necessary for innovation, creativity, and operational knowledge which leads to better decisions. You will then earn the R&R&R we all strive for.

CHAPTER 10

Listening is Serving

"To listen well is one part art and ninety-nine parts heart."
Jeff Gross

The core of Empowerment Leadership is giving away your power. One way you can give away your power is by listening in order to understand and not to respond. To be a better communicator, you need to stop talking and start listening. The next tip ties all the other tips together. Without caring enough to listen fully, you'll never become an Empowerment Leader.

Listening is Serving! I have to confess that I still struggle with being an effective listener. I am learning to listen and not to control the conversation. My poor listening skill is due to my insecurities. I also want to impress, am fearful of forgetting what I am going to say, and to be honest, just dealing with my 8-year-old self. I admit that I'm a recovering Jerk, but learning to listen well is at the core of being a powerful Empowerment Leader.

TIP #10

Learn to Listen Well

My wife tells me I'm not qualified to teach listening skills. My response to that is "what did you say?" Listening well is so important but so many of us struggle with it. I feel in grade school learning to listen should be right up there with the "3 R's" of education; Reading, 'Riting, and 'Rithmetic. I also feel that the onboarding program for any politician should include Listening Well training and they have to get an "A" to take office.

Our governmental Listening Well summer

makeup courses would be packed. Yet I digress. I feel that for me, and many others, to listen well is one part art and ninety-nine parts heart. We will learn the one part and ask your partners to help with the other ninety-nine.

In my Listen Well workshop (which is my best workshop but worst selling - no one listens), when I ask participants to share why listening is so important, they respond that listening well allows us to:

- See the world through other's eyes.

- Help people to seek us out for help.

- Create powerful relationships, full of trust, integrity, and mutual respect.

- Be effective communicators.

- Become better leaders.

- And my ultimate favorite, show we care.

Empowerment Leaders care and one way to show you care is by listening and showing empathy.

When we understand someone's needs, feelings, and thoughts we are building relationships, engaging fully with them, and including them. We are listening well.

Warren R. Miller in *Listening Well: The Art of Empathic Understanding* stated it well when he said, "accurate empathy is the ability to understand clearly what others are experiencing, to get them" and "accurate empathy clarifies communication and strengthens relationships." I couldn't agree more.

When we listen deeply not to reply but to "get them," we'll understand better what others are thinking, feeling, experiencing, and meaning. We need to change our mindset from being inwardly focused on what we are trying to get and become outwardly focused on what we want to give. We want to give them our full attention. We'll need to turn on our listening switch and have a willingness to listen well.

Richard, who worked for me, was one of the best listeners I ever knew. Not surprisingly, he is also a life coach. Once, I was in a meeting with him and I was in awe of how well he was listening to our client. He was listening with his whole body. You could feel how focused he was on wanting to understand our client's needs and the only words he would speak was an occasional "please tell me more." I now knew why

Richard was a 9-time Eagle Award winner for having the top sales in our company of over 400 sales engineers.

I personally was exhausted watching him because I wanted to interrupt, but knew he had this down and was in total control by just listening well. We, I mean he, had the willingness and ability to be an effective listener.

Miller states that to become a good listener, we need to understand some of the common roadblocks which redirect and interfere with the speaker that results in not fully understanding their intent. Roadblocks cause the speaker to stop what they were going to say, and causes them to go in another unintentional direction. We need to learn to avoid the roadblocks to listening well.

Common Roadblocks

Directing	Warning	Advising
Persuading	Moralizing	Judging
Agreeing	Shaming	Analyzing
Probing	Reassuring	Distracting

"To fully understand what someone is thinking and feeling, I have to fully understand what someone is saying."

Jeff Gross

In my own learning to listen well, it was a surprise to me that Advising, Persuading, Analyzing, Agreeing, and Probing were actual roadblocks to effective listening. I was greatly disappointed because I consider myself pretty good at all of them. I learned that to fully understand what someone is thinking and feeling, I have to fully understand what someone is saying. When we start giving advice, persuading them to think differently, analyzing their situation, probing them with questions, and even agreeing with them we will misdirect them into not fully communicating what they are thinking and more importantly feeling.

There are times when you will need to advise, persuade, analyze, agree, and probe but resist doing these until you have confirmation you fully understand the hidden message they are thinking and trying to communicate. Inserting a roadblock will cause them to drive around the roadblock in a different route than they planned. Leading them to miscommunicate what they are thinking or even worse, think that you don't care.

As an Empowerment Leader, we need to be careful not to become a roadblock. One of my favorite Will Rogers quotes is, "don't miss a good chance to shut up." On the top of my meeting notes before the meeting starts, I write "shut up and listen." So, in my own words, don't miss a good opportunity to "shut up and listen."

Once they are done speaking, get confirmation by stating, "I think what you are saying is _____. Is that correct, and is there anything else I should know?" Believe me, there is always more that you need to listen to. When they have stopped talking, wait a short pause to make sure, and then it's ok to ask questions. I recommend what I call the Three Laws of Asking Questions, which are:

Law I
Asking questions is not the same as listening

Law II
Do not ask more than three questions in a row

Law III
Better to ask open-ended then closed-ended questions

Law I is to remember to make sure the speaker has fully stopped talking and you have confirmed what they are thinking. Once you start your questions, you have become a roadblock so make sure the car has come to a complete stop. Law II is to avoid asking too many questions because it may come across as interrogating and judging. And lastly, Law III is to ask open-ended questions to flush out as much information as possible.

We also need to be mindful that the speaker may not be a good communicator and/or have fully thought out what they want to say. When we are going to be the one speaking in the conversation, we should write it out first, practice it, and do a mock conversation with a friend or co-worker. Far too often both sides are not properly prepared to speak well or listen well.

"Don't start solving, start listening."
Jeff Gross

One of the keys to listening well is to know how to listen when there is conflict. People tend to stop listening in conflict situations. As leaders, we need to avoid getting too emotional but rather do the unexpected and stay calm. Learn to take a deep breath and get the heart rate down before jumping in. Our goal in Empowerment Leadership is to listen to understand a different perspective, and to understand what matters most to someone else. Don't start solving, start listening.

Another tip in listening during conflict is to avoid the word "you" and replace it with "I". Personally, when someone uses the word "you" it is a trigger for my 8-year-old self to come alive and start swinging. I don't even know what is being said after the word "you". The metal gates go up and the listening stops.

Some examples of "you" vs "I":

You vs I

Your attitude is poor	vs	I feel that sometimes your attitude is poor
You didn't do that right	vs	I like when you do it this way
You're always late	vs	I'm frustrated when you're late

Rogers, Howieson, Neame have studied the neuroscience of using I-Language and found communicating perspectives using "I" were less hostile and open to resolution. Edward Kubany studied the effects of You-Language and, not surprisingly, determined it provoked anger. Subtly changing your habits of "you" to "I" statements will lead to better listening and speaking during times of conflict.

The importance of listening during conflict, or everyday conversations, at its core is serving. You are serving by listening well and respecting the speaker. This is the least we can do and is essential to becoming an Empowerment Leader. If you struggle like I do with listening, we'll need to own our faults and start listening better.

CHAPTER 11

But Wait There's More!

"Your ego blinds you to the truth that surrounds you."
Jeff Gross

Crazy, when you thought what else could there be to Empowerment Leadership there is more!

BONUS TIP #11

Hold yourself accountable by journaling

There is empowerment in writing down and analyzing your thoughts. Dr. David B. Feldman in *Power of Journaling* states that it can improve our happiness, goals attainment, and even physical health, and I want to add, our Empowerment Leadership skills. Olenda E. Johnson, at the United States Naval War College, in *Creating Space to Think: The What, Why, and How of Deliberate Reflection for Effective Leadership* states that journaling is a foundational component of leader development and:

- Causes self-awareness

- Improves team relationships

- Creates deeper understanding of experiences

- Helps with problem-solving

- Builds core values

- Enhances empathy

- Helps us know ourselves as a leader

- I'll also add a critical part of growing as an Empowerment Leader and holding ourselves accountable.

In my professional coaching, I stress the importance of weekly reflection to grow and hold ourselves accountable to being an Empowerment Leader. One of the questions to be explored in their journal is "are you deceiving yourself?" It is human nature to hear only what we want to hear. Our egos can be our largest hindrance to empowering our team. Your ego blinds you to the truth that surrounds you. Kept out of check, our ego will never allow us to know the power and greatness of Team Empowerment.

The three questions to reflect on weekly are:

1. What went well this week?

2. What could have gone better?

3. Did I deceive myself this week?

The first two questions are straight forward enough, but the third one is aimed at our egos. Did I deceive myself this week? Arrogance is the great deceiver of many so-called leaders. It tells us we are better than others and that we are superhuman. It creates an us-versus-them mentality and culture. One of exclusion and not inclusion.

The following are leadership experiences shared by two up-and-coming leaders I know very well. My awesome adult kids, Tabitha and Jacob.

CHAPTER 12

What NOT to do as an Empowerment Leader

> "I have yet to work for a leader who
> I wanted to model myself after."
> Tabitha Claus

Hi, Tabitha here! Yes, I'm Jeff and Maria's daughter and a young professional who has seen tremendous career success in just the nearly ten years since leaving college. Some of this is attributed to hard work, some to being in the right position at the right time, and lots is due to the leadership abilities I have been gifted by my family. Though I've had this success, I am a bit in awe that out of all the experiences I've had in this last decade, I have yet to work for a leader who I wanted to model myself after. Sad, I know, let's change that!

I've worked for a lot of bad bosses and have learned what I don't like as an employee and what I wanted to exemplify as an Empowerment Leader. In my team's most recent strategic planning retreat, I shared two professional and one personal attributes I loved about each of my team members. After I shared, they all decided they wanted to share something they appreciated about me. As I sat there listening to each team member share a characteristic about me, I was overwhelmed hearing them share things like "treats me like a human," "advocates for what our team needs," and "doesn't gatekeeper us from the rest of the organization." I thought to myself, these are characteristics that all leaders should have. I am not doing anything special, but just being the leader, I wished I had.

These were the characteristics of a leader I always craved to work under and here are my employees sharing how they see me as an authentic

Empowerment Leader. I see now, by working for awful bosses who micromanage and lead as a dictator, I have been able to take those poor leadership traits, flip them, and make sure I provide a better work experience for anyone I lead. Here is what I learned from the kinds of leaders young professionals are having to unlearn from.

The Micro-Boss

Don't you just love it when you're working hard on a project, trying to learn a new skill at work, or even just going about your day-to-day and you have your micromanager boss come over to you and proceed to make you feel like you have absolutely no idea what you're doing? You walk away from experiences like that doubting your abilities and second guessing if you're qualified to be doing your work. I worked in an environment where you never felt confident in the work you were doing because my boss always made me feel as if I wasn't capable of doing any work without their assistance and micro-oversight. The Micro-manager, or what we like to refer to as the Micro-Boss.

> "The tasks weren't difficult,
> but the management was."
> Tabitha Claus

A recent Gro-Nova poll resulted in 93% of us having worked for a Micro-Boss at one time or another. I started off my career supporting the executive team of a 350 million dollar community health center. It was a great place to start my career and learn about the administrative side of a large non-profit organization. My tasks were relatively easy and had great variety to them. A perfect place to start someone right out of college still trying to find where their career should go. The tasks weren't difficult, but the management was.

I had a Micro-Boss who was constantly looking over our shoulders, making sure we were doing the work we were tasked to do, seemingly for no reason. It was odd to me as I thought I was doing good work and that others in the same type of position as me were also doing good work, yet our boss was constantly making us second guess ourselves. I felt belittled, not trusted, and paranoid every day I worked under this Micro-Boss.

They couldn't give up the control and didn't have

the systems in place to better oversee and support us. We had no one-on-one meetings, just inconsistent check-ins as a group which resulted in constant looming of them around the office and the uneasy feeling, they were going to find yet, another thing we needed to do to "oversee" us on.

Looking back on working for this Micro-Boss, I see now that the micromanagement style really stemmed from their own lack of confidence as a manager. Indeed.com's article on "Why People Micromanage" stated that the common reasons bosses micromanage are:

- Loss of control over projects

- Unskilled employees on the team

- Belief that work deemed superior to their own may make them look inadequate

- Extreme need for control and domination

- Poor self-image and insecurities

- Inexperience in management

No matter the reasons, the Micro-Boss' fear drives them and their micro-oversight shows a total lack of trust and respect.

I think they felt like they always had to be on the lookout for what we were doing so that they could justify to their bosses that the team was productive and they were worth keeping on. They had no confidence in advocating for us, how we spent our time, or our abilities. But they lacked this confidence because they didn't have the systems in place to allow us to share with them what we needed as employees.

I learned from them the importance of allowing space for your employees to come to you to share what they are doing, what they need "your" help with, and then find the ways you can support and serve them.

I have weekly one-on-one meetings with all the employees I now serve. We start with personal check-ins, which help set the tone of what headspace they are coming into the meeting into, and then I ask "ok, what do you have for me?" Allowing them to bring up what they want to spend this time chatting about. In our Ten Tips to Empowerment Leadership workshop, we recommend that one-on-one meetings:

- Are no more than 30 minutes long

- Is the employee's meeting where they set the agenda

- Are an opportunity to build relationships

- Is a place where you listen first and speak last

Done right, one-on-one meetings will build relationships, emphasize empowerment, show that you care, and are an excellent opportunity to coach; all things to not be a Micro-Boss.

We end the one-on-one meeting with items I have for them, but oftentimes they have brought it up already. I really have seen this play out nicely and they hit every item I want to check in on already, even the concerns. This gives the team the autonomy to share what they need and prevents them from feeling like I'm micromanaging the conversation or their tasks. My team feels empowered by these weekly check-ins and I get a full picture of the impactful work my team is doing without feeling like or being a Micro-Boss.

The Dictator-Boss

Ok, ok, I know calling this next bad boss type a

'dictator' seems a bit aggressive, but as I was thinking of what to call this style of leadership, all I could think of was the "my way or no way," "no one makes a decision but me," "your ideas are never as good as mine" type of leader and dictator really sums that up nicely.

This type of boss has been the most challenging I've worked under. The dictator makes you feel pigeonholed and unable to move forward with your own work. They make it impossible for their teams to have autonomy and work on their own to move the organization forward. Simply, they lead by fear and oppression to ensure that their own ideas are the ones that matter and not that of their employees. Sounds like a dictator to me, how about you?

Have you ever had to muster up the courage to go speak to your boss about the simplest of requests? Like you had to take a few minutes to think about exactly what you were going to say, think about what kind of mood your boss seemed to be in, wait a few more minutes to think of how you'd respond to any of their questions, and then finally after passing by their office a couple times just to ensure now was the right time, you would go in and make your request? I hope very few of you have had this experience, but if you can relate then you've worked under a Dictator-Boss.

This was how every day felt like when I worked under my Dictator-Bosses - yes two! Looking back, they were fearful of not leading with fear because they were fearful of losing power, prestige, and control. What a waste of leadership potential and a waste of your employee's mental capacities and abilities. I've been working a lot on dismantling supremacy culture in my own team, and one of the characteristics is "Power-Hoarding", which I feel sums up portions of the Dictator-Boss. Empowerment Leaders give their power away to the team.

Those who hoard power assume they have the best interests of the organization at heart and assume those wanting change are ill-informed (stupid), emotional, and/or inexperienced (James & Okun, 2001). What a sad way to think about your employees.

The biggest thing I've learned from the power-hoarding structure I was working under, was finding ways to develop my team member's leadership skills. Making sure they have all the tools they need to do their tasks well and then providing them the space to do it. When you go in with a mindset that they aren't capable then you're automatically setting up your employees for failure. As Carol Dweck has researched, talents and abilities can be developed, boosting their achievement and performance (Dweck, 2009 & 2015).

Early on in my life, my dad taught me to be the 1 in 100 and the flipside of the 1 in 100 is those dang 99 in 100ers. The 99 in 100 people who will not step out of their comfort zones, not go above and beyond, and not take initiative to be and do better. Let me tell you, working for a 99 in 100er while being a 1 in 100 will drive you absolutely crazy.

By not being a Micro-Boss or Dictator-Boss and creating an environment where you're empowering your team and not diminishing them, I've seen employees go above and beyond my expectations and really take ownership of their duties. I've seen great collaboration between team members, team members thinking more creatively and feeling empowered to move forward with ideas and learn from the good and bad of those ideas. If that ain't Empowerment Leadership then nothing is.

Excuse me for one second...I'm back. I just had my first beautiful baby girl, Ripley. I'm a little tired and busy and I'll need to go now. So, as my Daddy told me a thousand times - emPOWER-ON!!

Tag Jacob! You're it. Moma-"SHIP", now that's leadership!

CHAPTER 13

Remote Working: The Perks and Pitfalls of Working at Home

"The best thing that happened to my work-life was COVID. Truly."
Jacob Gross

Hi, Jacob here! I started my first job in November 2019 right after finishing my Master's. It wasn't easy for me to find a job because I live in England and therefore need a visa from my employer. I had to apply to over 160 jobs, was only asked to sit for 11 interviews, and received 1 solitary offer. Needless to say, I took that offer.

The job was initially not very high paying, had me working weekends, and, oh, also had me doing a three-hour door-to-door commute three days a week that cost me around $500 a month. The first few months of my job were excruciating because of this. The frustrating commute and long days took their toll on me both physically and mentally. But I had to persist in it if I wanted to stay in England.

So, persist I did. Until a little thing called COVID hit in March 2020; you may have heard about it. This changed everything about my job. Now, I was no longer required to go to the office, so bye bye three-hour long, soul-crushing commute. This immediately took a huge weight off of my back. I'm sure I am not the only one who has flourished from the lack of office commute.

I found that my productivity increased tremendously as well since I no longer had to wake up at 5AM to go to the office and I no longer came home at 8PM. This allowed me to be more focused at work since I was able to get plenty of time for rest and relaxation. But it wasn't all smooth sailing.

There were some drawbacks when I switched to

a remote working lifestyle. First among them was finding a way to not go insane. Luckily for me, I was living with my partner so I had some company, but others who I worked with did not have that luxury. In England, when COVID first hit, we went into a heavy lockdown. I'm talking about not being able to legally leave the house for the entire summer unless you were going grocery shopping or going for a light walk around the block; and I mean **very** light walk.

> "When you are working with a remote team, it is vitally important to set up consistent meetings in order to connect with everyone."
>
> Jacob Gross

So, my company and I had to quickly adapt to this change and find ways to ensure that everyone was happy, healthy, and most importantly sane. Therefore, we set up consistent meetings to get everyone in the team involved and speak with one another. We started meeting once a day in the morning for a quick fifteen-minute standup in which we discussed what we worked on the day before, what we are going to do today, and how everyone is doing. The last part, in my opinion, was and is the most important aspect of these daily meetings. It allows everyone to be able to chat with one another and see how they are doing.

When you are working with a remote team, it is vitally important to set up consistent meetings in order to connect with everyone. In a normal office environment, this tends to occur naturally. You'll be walking to the office kitchen to refill your water or make a cup of tea, and oh there is Bill, let's see what Bill is up to. Unfortunately, when you start working from home, Bill is no longer in your house; or at least probably shouldn't be. So, to combat this change, you have to schedule these daily meetings in order to give everyone time to be able to discuss the work events of the day with one another and create a sense of community.

> "When your team is remote, consistency is key."
> Jacob Gross

As Tabitha also discussed, it is important to allow for one-on-one time between a leader and their employee. This can be a weekly or biweekly meeting which gives the leader time to ask how the employee is feeling in their job, the employee a space to voice any concerns, and the leader time to give feedback about how the employee is doing. This is even more important when remote.

Once again, in an office environment, this can tend to occur in a more natural way since the leader and employee are mandated to be in the same room as each other between the hours of nine to five; not so when the employee and leader can potentially be in different countries to one another. So, just as with the daily meetings, it is important to set up these consistent one-on-one meetings to allow both the leader and the employee to touch base.

Now, some of these things may already be implemented in your company even without remote working. However, when your team is remote, consistency is key. It is no longer as easy to miss a meeting because you know that you'll see Bill in the office later, and it is no longer as easy to ensure that the team is functioning properly both in a work sense and a mental health sense.

Another drawback I, and I'm sure many others, faced when starting to work remotely was how to still work with your teammates when they are scattered across the seven seas. Thankfully, we live in a time of technology that can make this easier to combat.

There are tools such as Zoom, Google Meet, and Skype to name a few which allow for a large number of people to join meetings and discuss their work with one another over video. This can immediately make a remote working space more sociable to a team since they can hear their teammates' voices and see their faces; whenever Bill decides to turn on his camera, of course.

Speaking of turning on your camera, I know that some people find it uncomfortable to have their cameras on. That is perfectly ok, and you should not try to force anyone to have their cameras on. They may have their family in the background, eating a well-deserved snack, or haven't gotten ready for the day yet. However, it does still help to be able to see the entire team. So, whenever possible, having cameras on in a video meeting can ensure that team members stay focused and that the team can see one another and not feel as isolated.

It is also important how you use video meetings. You shouldn't think of them as a tool that can only be used in strictly pre-setup meetings, but instead they can be seen as perfectly acceptable for quick, impromptu chats or longer work sessions between team members. This can allow the team to socialize with one another and be able to work on their tasks in a similar manner as when they were in an office together.

Tabitha adds: So important to build in that "water cooler" time for employees that gets lost when being remote. I start all of my meetings with about 10 minutes of socialization where I ask a silly question for the team to continue to get to know each other outside of their job duties. This has helped our dynamic as a remote team tremendously! Now, back to Jacob.

There are additional messaging tools that can be used to facilitate a remote team; such as Slack and Microsoft Teams to name a few more of them. These tools work in tandem to emails and allow for quick discussion and coordination between team members. Communicating via instant messages instead of email can allow for a remote team to stay up-to-date with one another and keep discussions organized between different teams in a company. It is also less formal and good for socialization and joking around with a teammate.

These tools can also be used in a more general sense in your company since they are extremely powerful in their ability to keep a large company organized. It can sometimes be difficult for people to sift through hundreds of emails, but when everything is automatically broken down into smaller bite-sized chunks, then it can be much easier for team members to stay on top of things.

> "Remote working is here to stay."
> Jacob Gross

Now, some of you may be saying that this sounds all nice and acceptable when COVID was in full swing, but now that we are returning to a more normal situation, remote working can be put to rest. However, remote working is here to stay. People have gotten used to having this new work-life integration in which they no longer have to commute for hours on end, have their boss peering over their shoulder, or be forced to talk to Bill about his five cats each day. They are now used to waking up at a more normal hour, keeping the extra money in their pockets instead of paying for their commute each day, and being able to be home in time for dinner.

Alex Noah at The Next Tech wrote in *Top 10*

Benefits of Remote Work for Businesses in 2022 that companies can benefit by having:

- Improvements in Productivity

- Reduced Equipment Costs

- Lower employee turnover (put my name in this benefit)

- Lower Office Rentals

- Access to a wider talent pool

- Flexibility in work hours

- A Healthier Workforce

- A global workforce at all levels

"We need to be measured by the results of our work and not where the work is being done."
Jacob Gross

I know that I, and once again, I'm sure many others will agree with me, would leave their current job if they were forced to come back to the office full time; especially since many progressive companies offer hybrid remote work options. Morgan Smith at CNBC reported that 64% of workers would consider quitting if asked to return to the office full-time.

Luckily, and wisely, my company has chosen to allow a hybrid remote work policy. Both Senior and Junior management are supportive and also working remotely. Some people of course would and do prefer to work in the office, but enough of us have seen the other side and can confirm that the grass is indeed greener.

Now, it doesn't need to be an "us vs them" type of a situation where the company feels like they desperately need everyone to come back to the office and the employees feel like they need to quit their jobs to keep working from home. I hope that I've shown how to be able to manage a remote team better and ensure that all parties are kept happy.

Also, there are even some nice financial incentives for a company to not insist that everyone comes back to the office. For instance, my fiancée's father's company decided to stop paying for an extra floor of office space since they determined that not enough people were coming back to the office. This immediately cut the overhead that they were paying and allowed the employees to know that their company isn't expecting all of them to come back to the office.

As I previously mentioned, many people find that they can be more productive when they are working from home. They can work exactly how they want to, singing pop songs in the middle of the day and all, and they can stay more refreshed and less stressed by cutting their commute time. This therefore allows them to produce higher quality work which is beneficial to both the employee and the company as a whole. We need to be measured by the results of our work and not where the work is being done. All the team has to do is make some few changes and stay consistent with those changes and everyone is happily working from home with great results.

The Last Thought

"As a leader, we own the well-being of the people we are blessed with, and have the responsibility to serve them."
Jeff Gross

Polls after polls are telling us that our teams are not fully engaged, unhappy, and looking to leave because of us. We can go into the office, or log in remotely, see the false smiling faces of our team, and bury our heads in the top drawer of our desk wishing the problems of low engagement, high turnover, and poor job satisfaction would just fix themselves.

That will not change the fact that, as a leader we

own the well-being of the people we are blessed with, and have the responsibility to serve them; not as a Micro-Boss or a Dictator-Boss, but as an Empowerment Leader. Transplanting your old selfish, self-serving heart with a new heart of service, will result in an Empowerment Culture with happier and more productive people who will never want to leave you.

Maria, Tabitha, Jacob, and I hope we have changed your heart and given you the tools to be an Empowerment Leader. So go forth Empowerment Leaders, and

emPOWER ON!

About the Family of Authors

We are a family of leaders and believe everyone is a leader in their own spheres of influence. Whether a mother, father, sister, brother, CEO, or janitor, we all have leadership opportunities to positively influence someone's life.

Jeff Gross is the Chief Empowerment Officer of Gro-Nova Inc. He has over 20 years of leadership experience working for Fortune 500 companies and small-to-medium sized businesses. He has an MBA and a BS in Engineering.

Dr. Maria Gross has a Doctorate in Leadership and is the wife and empowerment partner of Jeff for over 33 years. She also has a BS in Engineering and is a Professor in Education.

Tabitha (Gross) Claus is the daughter of Jeff and Maria and is leading a team as the Director of Development of a large non-profit organization in Seattle, Washington. She has a BBA in Management and Human Resources.

Jacob Gross, the son of Jeff and Maria, has a Master's in Astrophysics from University of Cambridge, England and is a DevOps Engineer for a large transportation company.

REFERENCES

Alshammari, A., Almutairi, N. N., & Thuwaini, S. F. (2015). Ethical leadership: The effect on employees. *International Journal of Business and Management*, *10*(3), 108.

Alex Noah (2022). Top 10 Benefits of Remote Work for Businesses in 2022. https://www.the-next-tech.com/business/top-10-benefits-of-remote-work-for-businesses-in-2022/

Bakke, D. (2021), The Decision Maker: Unlock the Potential of Everyone in Your Organization. Pear Press.

Blanchard, K. & Hodges, P. (2003), The Servant Leader: Transforming Your Heart, Head, Hands and Habits. Raj Sisodia – Servant Leadership Conscious Leadership. Nashville Tennessee: Thomas Nelson.

BranchED (2021). BranchED Tool for Critical Reflection for Teacher Educators. https://drive.google.com/file/d/1tlyhHbvbSrOS1144d0uLAZzNohX4Kib8/view

Burton, J. (2007) The Business Case for a Healthy Workplace, Industrial Accident Prevention Association, UMass Lowel. https://www.uml.edu/docs/fd_business_case_healthy_workplace_tcm18-42671.pdf

Dweck, C. S. (2009). Mindsets: Developing talent through a growth mindset. *Olympic Coach, 21*(1), 4-7.

Dweck, C. (2015). Carol Dweck revisits the growth mindset. *Education week, 35*(5), 20-24.

Feldman, D. B., Ph.D. (2009), The Power of Journaling: Can journaling help us cope during troubled times? Psychology Today https://www.psychologytoday.com/us/blog/supersurvivors/202009/the-power-journaling

Harter, J. (2018), Employee Engagement on the Rise in the U.S. gallup.com. https://news.gallup.com/poll/241649/employee-engagement-rise.aspx

Howard, T. C. (2003). Culturally relevant pedagogy: Ingredients for critical teacher reflection. *Theory into practice, 42*(3), 195-202.

Indeed Editorial Team (2021), Why Do People Micromanage? (Plus, How To Respond to a Micromanager). Indeed.com https://www.indeed.com/career-advice/career-development/micromanagement

Indeed.com (2022), Conducting Stay Interviews: Three Questions to Ask. Indeed.com https://www.indeed.com/hire/c/info/conducting-stay-interviews?gclid=CjwKCAjw46CVBhB1EiwAgy6M4rIp0PqzLoqQ1pSB-U3v_B8lA0AU9uC-brQmqNaEXZ9pmhm4ysaxrBoCyRIQAvD_BwE&aceid=

Jones, K., & Okun, T. (2001). White supremacy culture. *Dismantling racism: A workbook for social change.*

Jensen, S.M. & Luthans, F. (2006), Entrepreneurs as Authentic Leaders: Impact on Employees' Attitudes. Leadership & Organization Development Journal.

Johnson, O.E. (2020), Creating Space to Think: The What, Why, and How of Deliberate Reflection for Effective Leadership. The Journal of Character &

Leadership Development.

Kearl, B. (2018), The Onboarding Checklist That Puts Culture First. BambooHR https://www.glassdoor.com/employers/blog/onboarding-checklist-culture/

Kubany, E.S. (1992), Verbalized Anger and Accusatory "You" Messages as Cues for Anger and Antagonism among Adolescents. Adolescence https://eric.ed.gov/?id=EJ451193

Miller, W. R. (2018), Listening Well: The Art of Empathic Understanding.

Mochari, I. (2013), The One Meeting That Will Help You Keep Your Top Employees. Inc. https://www.inc.com/ilan-mochari/stay-interviews.html

Morgan Smith (2022), 64% of workers would consider quitting if asked to return to the office full-time. CNBC. https://www.cnbc.com/2022/04/28/64percent-of-workers-would-consider-quitting-if-asked-to-return-to-office-full-time.html

Offermann, L. R., & Hellmann, P. S. (1996). Leadership behavior and subordinate stress: A 360" view. *Journal of occupational health psychology*, 1(4), 382.

Paul, K. Ph.D (2016), Sustaining Employee Engagement and Job Satisfaction. SHRM
https://www.shrm.org/hr-today/trends-and-forecasting/special-reports-and-expert-views/pages/karen-paul.aspx?_ga=2.181175584.680336627.1661183761-422095082.1661183761

Phillips, K.W. (2014), How Diversity Makes Us Smarter. Scientific American
https://www.scientificamerican.com/article/how-diversity-makes-us-smarter/

Raypole, C. (2021), You're Not a Fraud. Here's How to Recognize and Overcome Imposter Syndrome. healthline.com
https://www.healthline.com/health/mental-health/imposter-syndrome

Rogers, S. L., Howieson, J. & Neame, C. (2018), I understand you feel that way, but I feel this way: the benefits of I-language and communicating perspective during conflict. PeerJ https://www.ncbi.nlm.nih.gov/pmc/articles/PMC5961625/

Sullivan, J. (2013), Stay Interviews: 20 Possible Questions You Should Consider Asking. TNLT Talent Management. https://www.tlnt.com/stay-interviews-20-possible-questions-you-should-consider-asking/

Printed in Great Britain
by Amazon